STATE AND LOCAL GOVERNMENTS: GROWING FISCAL CHALLENGES

STATE AND LOCAL GOVERNMENTS: GROWING FISCAL CHALLENGES

U.S. GOVERNMENT ACCOUNTABILITY OFFICE

Nova Science Publishers, Inc.
New York

LIBRARY OF CONGRESS CATALOGING-IN-PUBLICATION DATA
State and local governments : growing fiscal challenges / GAO, author.
p. cm.
ISBN 978-1-60456-585-0 (softcover)
1. Finance, Public--United States--States. 2. Intergovernmental fiscal relations--United States. 3. Local finance--United States. I. United States. Government Accountability Office.
HJ275.S683 2008
336'.01373--dc22
2008015604

Published by Nova Science Publishers, Inc. ✢ New York

CONTENTS

PREFACE*

In speeches and presentations over the past several years, I have called attention to our large and growing federal fiscal challenge and the risks it poses to our nation's future. For over a decade, the U.S. Government Accountability Office (GAO) has run long-term simulations showing that absent a change in policy, the combined effects of demographic changes and growing health care costs drive ever-increasing federal deficits and debt levels. GAO's most recent federal simulations show an anticipated persistent gap between expected revenues and expected spending resulting in a very large and growing federal debt burden over time. The primary drivers of the spending are large federal entitlement programs—Medicare, Medicaid, and Social Security. Spending on health care programs (Medicare and Medicaid) in particular represents the fastest growing and most immediate problem. I have repeatedly warned that the current fiscal path of the federal government is "imprudent and unsustainable."

Fiscal sustainability presents a national challenge shared by all levels of government. The federal government and state and local governments share in the responsibility of fulfilling important national goals, and these subnational governments rely on the federal government for a significant portion of their revenues. As happens at the federal level, these subnational governments may also face serious fiscal stress in the future. To provide Congress and the public with a broader perspective on our nation's fiscal outlook, GAO has developed a fiscal model of the state and local sector. This unique model enables GAO to simulate fiscal outcomes for the entire state and local government sector for several decades into the future.

---

* Excerpted from GAO-08-317, dated January 2008.

The findings of these new simulations indicate that the state and local government sector faces fiscal challenges that in many ways mirror those of the federal government. In particular, GAO has found that in the absence of policy changes, large and recurring fiscal challenges for the state and local sector will begin to emerge within a decade. For example, the analysis suggests that state and local governments will need to somewhat increase their pension contributions to fully fund pension costs for their employees. Additionally, there is increasing concern that investment in the nation's infrastructure is not sufficient to maintain its condition and to accommodate the increased demand of a growing economy. Moreover, as in the federal sector, the growth in health-related costs serves as the primary driver of the fiscal challenges facing the state and local government sector. In particular, two types of state and local expenditures will likely rise quickly because of escalating medical costs. The first is Medicaid expenditures, and the second is the cost of health insurance for state and local employees and retirees. At the same time, most revenue growth is expected to remain roughly flat as a percentage of Gross Domestic Product. As such, the projected rise in health-related costs is the root of the fiscal difficulties these simulations suggest will occur.

Addressing the nation's long-term fiscal imbalances constitutes a major challenge for all levels of government. There are no "quick fixes," and all levels of government need to work in tandem to address the complex and interrelated reforms that need to be made. Continuing on this unsustainable path will gradually erode, and ultimately damage, our economy, our standard of living, and potentially our domestic tranquility and national security. This is a challenge that needs to be addressed with a greater sense of urgency by policymakers since time is currently working against us.

State and local governments provide an array of services to their residents, such as primary and secondary education, libraries, police and fire services, social programs, roads and other infrastructure, public colleges and universities, and more. These subnational governments may face fiscal stress similar to the federal government. Given the nature of the partnership among levels of government in providing services to Americans and the economic interrelationships among levels of government, understanding potential future fiscal conditions of the state and local government sector is important for federal policymaking. To provide Congress and the public with this broader context, we developed a fiscal model of the state and local sector. This report describes this model and provides (1) simulations of the state and local government sector's long-term fiscal outlook, (2) an analysis of the underlying causes of potential fiscal difficulties for the sector, (3) a discussion of the extent to which the long-term simulations are sensitive to alternative assumptions, and (4) an examination of how the state and local government sector could add to future federal fiscal challenges.[1]

To develop these long-term simulations, we developed a state and local model that projects the level of receipts and expenditures of the sector in future years based on current and historical spending and revenue patterns. Key categories of receipts for state and local governments include several types of state and local taxes (e.g., personal income, sales, property, and corporate), income on assets owned by the sector (e.g., financial assets), and grants from the federal government. Categories of expenditures include wages and salaries, health insurance, and pension costs of state and local employees (e.g., teachers and police); payments of social benefits (e.g., Medicaid, unemployment); depreciation expense on state and local capital stock; interest payments on state and local financial debt; and other expenditures of the sector.

The potential fiscal outcomes of the state and local government sector are projected through two fiscal balance measures: net lending or borrowing and what we call the operating balance. Net lending or borrowing—which is roughly analogous to the federal unified surplus or deficit[2]—is a measure of the balance of all receipts and expenditures during a given time frame. Historically, total expenditures have usually exceeded total receipts, and the sector issues debt to cover part of the costs of its capital projects. As such, net lending or borrowing typically measures the need for the sector to borrow funds or draw down assets to cover its expenditures. The operating balance net of funds for capital expenditures—referred to in this report as the "operating balance"—is a measure of the ability of the sector to cover its current expenditures out of current receipts, that is, the balance of expenditures and receipts related to activities taking place in a given year. Most states have some sort of requirement to balance operating budgets. Projects with longer time frames are typically budgeted separately from the operating budgets and financed by a combination of current receipts, federal grants, and the issuance of debt. Because some current receipts may be used to fund part of longer-term investments, we developed a measure of the operating balance that makes adjustments for the extent to which current receipts are unavailable to fund current expenditures because they have been spent on longer-term projects, such as investments in buildings and roads.

We developed a "base case" simulation in which we assume that the current set of policies in place across federal, state, and local governments remains constant. In other words, we assume that the tax structure is not changed in the future and that current policies regarding the provision of government services remain the same.[3] The primary data source for the model is the National Income and Product Accounts (NIPA) developed by the Bureau of Economic Analysis, U.S. Department of Commerce. The state and local model examines the aggregate fiscal outcomes for the sector and does not examine the condition of any individual state or local government. The time frame for the simulations extends until 2050, paralleling our federal fiscal model. The two models are designed such that they can be combined to examine the entire U.S. government sector. Appendix I contains our overall methodology, which provides a detailed discussion of the assumptions underlying the projections, the measurement of these fiscal balances, and the sources of data. Appendix II provides a discussion of estimates of future income on assets owned by the sector and interest paid on the sector's debt. Appendix III provides a discussion of the development of the model's treatment of pension and retiree and employee health care costs. Appendix IV provides all of the model equations, and appendix V provides variable definitions.

RESULTS IN BRIEF

Our model shows that in less than a decade the state and local government sector will begin to face growing fiscal challenges. Both fiscal balance measures (1) net lending or borrowing and (2) the operating balance—are likely to remain within their historical ranges in the next few years, but both begin to decline thereafter and fall below their historical ranges within a decade. That is, absent policy changes, state and local governments will face an increasing gap between receipts and expenditures in the coming years. Since most state and local governments actually face requirements that their operating budgets be balanced or nearly balanced in most years, the declining fiscal conditions our simulations suggest are really just a foreshadowing of the extent to which these governments will need to make substantial policy changes to avoid these potential growing fiscal imbalances.

As is true for the federal sector, the growth in health-related expenditures is the primary driver of the fiscal challenges facing the state and local government sector. In particular, two types of state and local expenditures will likely rise quickly. The first is Medicaid expenditures, and the second is expenditures by these governments for health insurance for state and local employees and retirees. Conversely, other types of expenditures of state and local governments in the aggregate—such as wages and salaries of state and local workers, nonhealth transfer payments (e.g., family assistance), and investments in capital goods—are assumed to grow slower than gross domestic product (GDP). Moreover, under the current policy scenario of the base case, most revenue categories grow at approximately the same rate as GDP. Therefore, the projected rise in health-related expenditures is the root of the fiscal difficulties these simulations suggest will occur. Although health care expenditures clearly appear to be a looming problem for the state and local government sector, the extent of fiscal difficulties faced by any given state or local government will vary with its individual expenditure and tax profile.

We also used the model to examine how the fiscal balance measures would be affected over the long-term under assumptions that differed from those of our base case. In particular, we analyzed scenarios that differ across three factors: (1) the rate of growth in tax receipts, (2) the rate of growth in expenditures, and (3) the rate of growth in medical care expenditures. Some of the alternative scenarios were designed to examine the extent to which a change in base-case assumptions for any of these factors would enable the state and local government sector to maintain fiscal balances in their historical ranges. We found that it would be difficult to address the expected future fiscal deficits solely through tax increases or solely through expenditure cuts.

Since 1992, we have produced long-term simulations of what might happen to federal deficits and debt under various policy scenarios. Our most recent long-term federal simulations show ever larger deficits resulting in a very large and growing federal debt burden over time.[4] In that work, we found that federal fiscal difficulties stem primarily from an expected explosion of health-related expenditures. Our findings thus show that the state and local sector will provide an additional drag on an already declining federal government fiscal outlook and that the critical problem of escalating costs of health care is an economywide problem that will need to be addressed by all levels of government.

Chapter 1

BACKGROUND

The state and local government sector consists of 50 state governments and 87,525 local governments. These local governments include 3,034 county governments, 19,429 municipal governments, 16,504 townships, 13,506 school districts, and 35,052 special districts.[5] State and local governments provide vital services to citizens such as law enforcement, public education, and sewage treatment. Local governments derive their authority from the states, and the powers and responsibilities granted to local governments vary considerably. For example, while states generally provide authority to local governments to tax real property, local governments vary in their authority to levy other types of taxes, such as personal income or sales taxes.

State and local governments collect receipts and receive federal funds to provide services to their constituents. In 2006, state and local governments received $1.9 trillion in total receipts. Taxes, such as property taxes, sales and excise taxes, personal income tax, and corporate income taxes, make up a large component of these receipts—fully $1.2 trillion. In addition, the federal government provided over $400 billion to state and local governments in the form of various grants (including Medicaid), loans, and loan guarantees. These federal funds accounted for approximately 22 percent of state and local government total receipts. State and local governments also obtain revenues from several other sources, such as income receipts on financial assets; certain receipts from businesses and individuals (such as vehicle and licensing fees); and, in some years, from surpluses on government-run enterprises that provide services such as energy, liquor, lotteries, and public transit.

State and local governments fund a broad range of services such as public safety, housing, education, and public transportation programs. In 2006, state and local governments spent $691 billion on education—the largest expenditure category for the sector. These governments also spent $263 billion on projects such as highways, public transit, agriculture, and natural resources, and $242 billion on public safety services such as police and fire departments as well as prisons. State and local governments also provide a broad range of other services, such as income security for the poor and disabled, health-related services, housing and community development, recreation services such as parks, and utilities such as water, sewage, and energy.

Budget processes vary considerably across the 50 states. According to the National Association of State Budget Officers (NASBO), about half of states enact budgets annually, while most others enact biennial budgets, and a few undertake a mix of annual and biennial budgeting. Most states budget separately for current operating costs and capital expenditures. The capital budget is used for states' capital projects, and states frequently issue debt to help fund these investments. Most states have some form of balanced budget requirement for general funds—the fund that covers current operating costs—but the nature of these balanced budget requirements varies considerably. For example, some states require governors to submit a balanced budget, while others mandate that legislatures pass a balanced budget. Some direct governors to sign a balanced budget, and some require governors to execute a balanced budget. Many of the balanced budget provisions allow states to run small, short-term deficits.

Chapter 2

THE STATE AND LOCAL GOVERNMENT SECTOR'S FISCAL DIFFICULTIES ARE LIKELY TO EMERGE WITHIN THE NEXT 10 YEARS

Our base case model rests on certain key assumptions. In particular, in the base case we assume that current federal, state, and local policies remain constant. On the receipt side, this translates into an assumption that the current tax structures of state and local governments are maintained in future years and that tax receipt growth reflects past experience, except that we remove the effect of past policy changes and the effects of unusual capital gains.[6] On the expenditure side, we make assumptions that would generally be consistent with the maintenance of current policies in the provision of services to citizens. Since compensation of state and local employees is a large cost component of providing services to citizens, our assumptions about the growth in the number of state and local employees over time, as well as the growth in their wages, are significant components through which we implement the assumptions of the maintenance of current policy. Since 1980, the level of employment in the state and local sector has grown significantly faster than the U.S. population, but for our simulation we maintain state and local government employment as a steady share of the population over time. This would be consistent with the maintenance of current policy if there were no productivity gains in the sector, or a modest increase in real services, to the extent that state and local workers experience gains in productivity.[7] Also, we assume that employees of state and local governments receive pay increases each year equal to those of private sector workers—an assumption that is generally consistent with historical experience.[8] Finally, we assume that the total cost of many goods procured by the sector to provide services will rise with increases in the population being served and the rate of inflation in the economy. Table 1 summarizes the assumptions of the base case model.

Table 1. Base Case Model Assumptions

Type of receipt or expenditure		Assumption
Receipts	Taxes	Historical experience net of policy changes and unusual capital gains used to determine how taxes will grow over time; maintains current tax structure.
	Federal grants	Medicaid grant projections from Congressional Budget Office's (CBO) intermediate case[a] for all simulation years, other grants from CBO for the next 10 years. After 10 years these grants grow with population and economywide inflation.
Expenditures	Compensation of state and local workers	Assume workforce grows at the same rate as the growth in population, and state/local wage growth is same as private-sector wage growth (as projected by CBO).
	Pension contributions	Develop estimate of steady rate of employer contributions to fully fund promised pensions (see app. III for more details).
	Health insurance cost for employees and retirees	Estimated pay-as-you-go expenditures on health insurance (see app. III for more details).
	Medicaid expenditures of state governments	Rise in state Medicaid expenditures is based on the same projections as CBO's intermediate projections for growth in federal Medicaid grants to states.
	Nonhealth expenditures	These expenditures grow with population and economywide inflation.

[a] CBO provides an intermediate case projection for Medicaid costs and a faster and slower growing projection.

Source: GAO analysis.

We calculated two measures of fiscal balance for the state and local government sector for each year until 2050. The measures are:

- Net lending or borrowing—the balance of all receipts and expenditures during a given time frame. This indicates the need for the sector to borrow funds or draw down assets to cover its expenditures. This measure is roughly analogous to the federal unified surplus or deficit.

- Operating balance net of funds for capital expenditures—or simply the "operating balance"—a measure of the ability of the sector to cover its current expenditures out of current receipts. In developing this measure we subtract funds used to finance longer-term projects—such as investments in buildings and roads—from receipts since these funds would not be available to cover current expenses. (See app. I for more detail on the measurement of this balance).

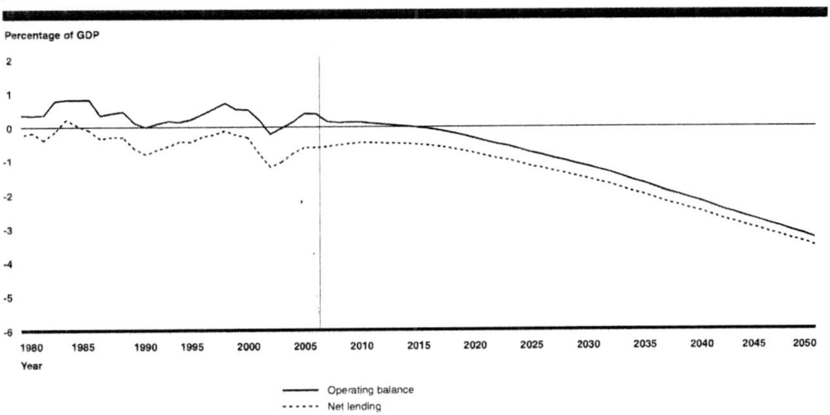

Sources: Historical data from NIPA and GAO analysis.

Figure 1. Balance Measures for State and Local Model, as a Percentage of GDP.

Figure 1 shows values of the two balance measures—net lending or borrowing and operating balance—as a percentage of GDP under our base-case assumptions. Historical data from 1980 to 2006 are shown along with our model simulations beginning in 2007 and running through 2050. The figure shows that the two measures generally track one another. It also shows that, historically, net lending or borrowing has typically been negative, but rarely by more than 1 percent of GDP. This indicates that the sector generally issues debt—primarily to fund capital expenditures—but has done so at a reasonably stable pace. Additionally, the operating balance measure has historically been positive most of the time, ranging from about zero to about 1 percent of GDP. Thus, the sector usually has been able to cover its current expenses with incoming receipts. But the simulation suggests that while projected balances for both net lending or borrowing and the operating balance remain in their historical ranges for the next several years, the balances will soon begin to decline and will fall below their historical ranges within a decade. That is, the model suggests that the state and local government sector will face increasing fiscal stress in just a few years. Our simulations also indicate that by the mid-2020s the balance measures will both be well below their historical ranges, and will continue to fall throughout the remainder of the simulation time frame. These projected deficits—worsening throughout the projection time frame under an unchanged policy scenario—indicate that, because most state and local governments cannot actually run such deficits for any length of time, these governments will need to make tough choices on spending and tax policy to meet their budget requirements and to promote favorable bond ratings.

Another way of measuring the long-term challenges faced by the state and local sector is through a measure known as the "fiscal gap." With deficits rising rapidly as shown in figure 1, the outstanding debt of the state and local sector will experience unprecedented growth. The fiscal gap is an estimate of the action needed today and maintained for each and every year to achieve fiscal balance over a certain period. We measured the gap as the amount of spending reduction or tax increase needed to maintain debt as a share of GDP at or below today's ratio.[9] For the state and local sector, we calculated that to close the fiscal gap would require action today equal to a 15.2 percent tax increase or a 12.9 percent reduction in spending financed by non-grant revenues. The fiscal gap can also be expressed as a share of the economy or in present value dollars. We calculated that in 2007 dollars the fiscal gap amounts to $10.6 trillion, which represents 1.4 percent of the discounted value of GDP over the same time frame.

Chapter 3

DECLINE IN FISCAL BALANCES IS RELATED TO RAPIDLY GROWING HEALTH-RELATED COSTS

Based on our review of the evidence, we estimate that expenditure growth for health care will be significant and these expenditures will constitute a rapidly growing burden for state and local governments. Two types of state and local expenditures in particular will likely rise quickly due to escalating medical costs. First, under CBO's intermediate projections, federal Medicaid grants to states per recipient will rise by 1 percent more than GDP per capita in the coming years.[10] Since Medicaid is a federal and state program with federal Medicaid grants based on a matching formula, these estimates indicate that expenditures for Medicaid by state governments will rise quickly as well. Second, we estimated future expenditures for health insurance for state and local employees and retirees. Specifically, we assume that the excess cost factor—the growth in these health care costs per capita above GDP per capita—will average 1.4 percentage points per year through 2035 and then begin to decline, reaching 0.6 percent by 2050.[11] This results in a rapidly growing burden from these health-related activities in state and local budgets. In contrast, our implementation of assumptions about current policies indicated that, in aggregate, other expenditure categories grow less than GDP in our base-case simulations.[12] For example, even though the wages and salaries of primary and secondary education employees are a large expenditure of the state and local sector, under our base-case assumptions these costs are not expected to grow any faster than the rate of growth of the general economy and will not represent an increasing burden on governments relative to their revenues.[13] These base-case assumptions differ from historical experience in which real spending on primary and secondary education per pupil has risen in the past few decades. If such a trend were to continue, spending on education could place a growing burden on state and local governments in future years. Figure 2 shows the projected expenditures of the sector as a percentage of GDP.

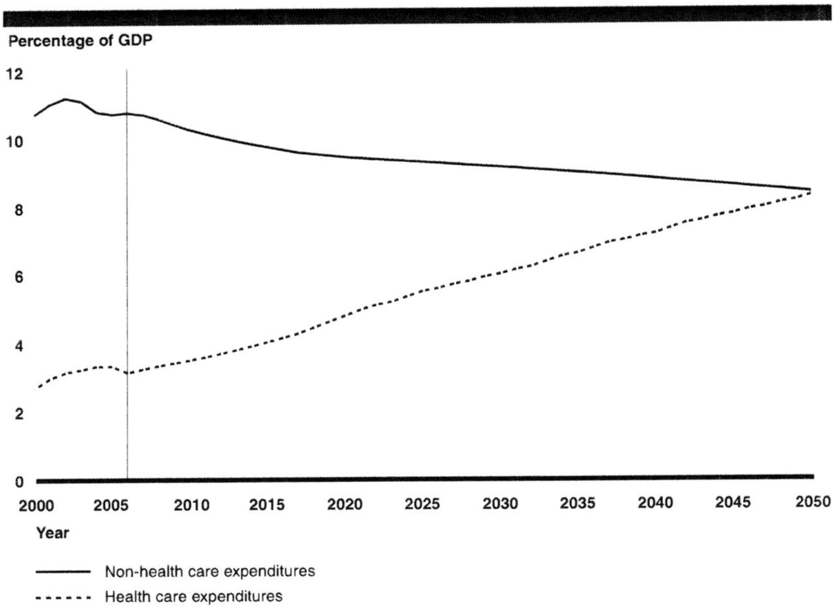

Note: Health care expenditures include health care benefits for employees and retirees and medical spending on behalf of other individuals, such as Medicaid and the State Children's Health Insurance Program (SCHIP) (a children's health care program); Nonhealth care expenditures include all expenditures with the exception of health care and interest payments.

Sources: Historical data from NIPA and GAO analysis.

Figure 2. State and Local Government Expenditures, as a Percentage of GDP.

On the receipt side, state and local governments impose a variety of taxes. Our model projections suggest that most of these tax receipts will show modest growth in the future—and some are projected to experience a modest decline—relative to GDP. Figure 3 shows the expected path of several tax revenue sources. We found that personal state income taxes will show a small rise relative to GDP in coming years. This likely reflects that some state governments have a small degree of progressivity in their income tax structures. Sales taxes of the sector are expected to experience a slight decline as a percentage of GDP in the coming years. Property taxes—which are mostly levied by local governments—should rise slightly as a share of GDP in the future. These differential tax growth projections indicate that any given jurisdiction's tax revenue prospects may be uniquely tied to the composition of taxes it imposes.

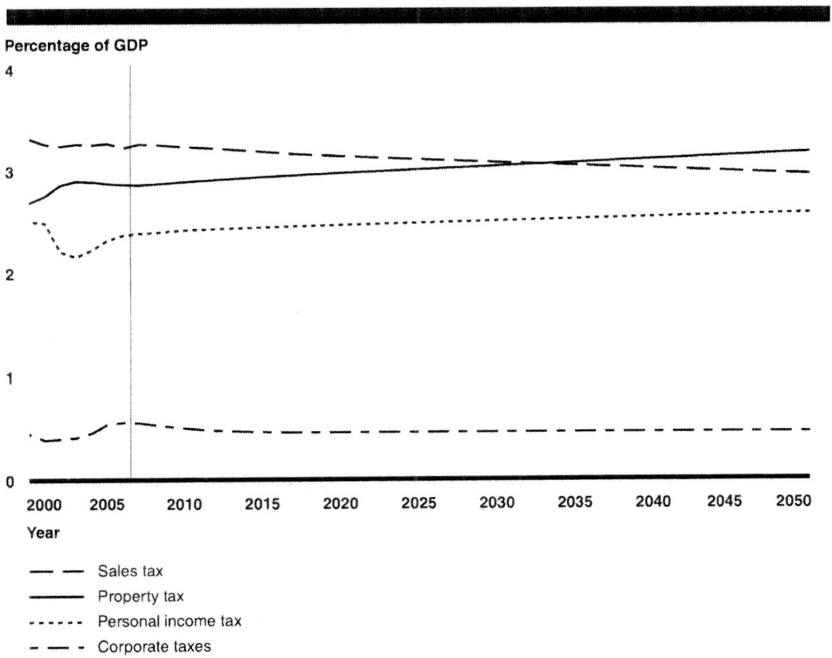

Sources: Historical data from NIPA and GAO analysis.

Figure 3. State and Local Government Tax Receipts, as a Percentage of GDP.

The only source of revenue we expect to grow rapidly is federal grants to state governments for Medicaid. However, since Medicaid is a matching formula grant program, the projected escalation in federal Medicaid grants simply reflects expected increased Medicaid expenditures that will be shared by state governments. That is, we assume that current policy remains in place and the shares of Medicaid expenditures borne by the federal government and the states remain unchanged. Federal grants unrelated to Medicaid are projected, based on CBO analysis, to decline somewhat relative to GDP in the coming years.[14]

Chapter 4

SUBSTANTIAL POLICY CHANGES WOULD BE NEEDED TO PREVENT THE FISCAL DECLINE IN THE STATE AND LOCAL GOVERNMENT SECTOR

We developed several scenarios with alternative assumptions to better understand the sensitivity of our results. For these analyses, we focused on the operating balance measure because this is a proxy for the operating budgets that most state and local governments have requirements to generally keep in balance. The assumptions varied in these alternative scenarios include (1) the growth of tax receipts, (2) the growth in state and local expenditures, and (3) the rate of growth in health care costs.

Tax Receipts Would Need to Rise Considerably Faster than Historical Experience to Enable the Operating Balance to Remain in Historical Range

In the base-case model, we assume that current policy, such as tax rates and structures, will remain unchanged. We also modeled alternative scenarios with different assumptions about the growth rate of tax receipts. In the first alternative, we use the historical growth of tax revenues for the sector since 1980. The second alternative is a "maintain balance" scenario in which we assume that taxes are raised to whatever level would be required to maintain a nonnegative operating balance in every year of the simulation. Figure 4 shows the tax growth path for the base case and two alternative scenarios.

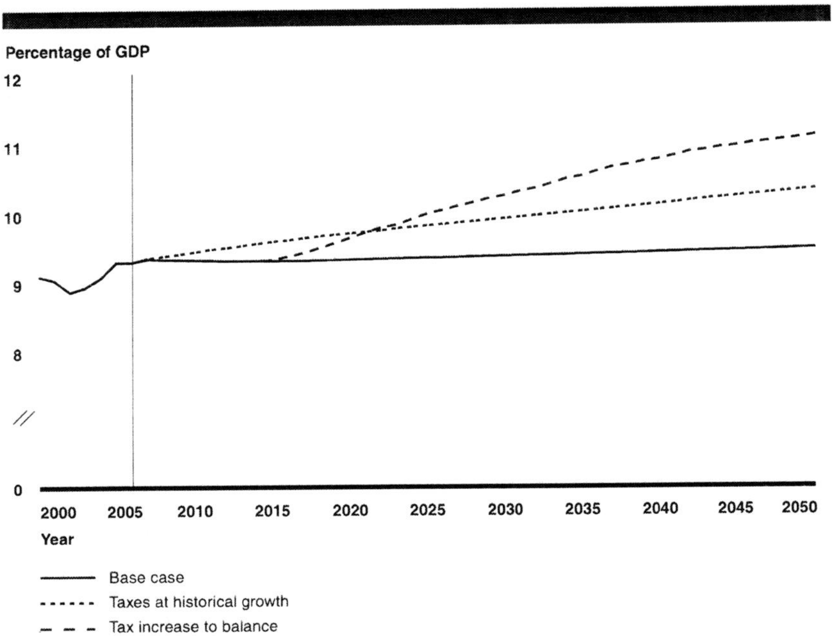

Note: Historical data are from 2000–2006. Projections are from 2007–2050.

Figure 4. Alternative Growth Scenarios: Tax Receipts, as a Percentage of GDP.

Under the base case, we found that aggregate tax revenues for the entire state and local sector will likely remain about a constant percentage of GDP. In the historical growth scenario, receipts would rise somewhat in the future relative to GDP. For the "maintain balance" scenario, tax receipts need to rise considerably faster than under either of the other cases to fulfill the requirements of the scenario. In fact, by 2050, state and local taxes as a percentage of GDP would have to rise by about 17 percent above the base case to avoid fiscal deficits. In other words, it would take a substantial increase in taxes—a considerably faster increase than that experienced historically—to maintain a nonnegative operating balance solely through increased taxes.

STATE AND LOCAL EXPENDITURES WOULD NEED TO BE CUT SUBSTANTIALLY TO MAINTAIN FISCAL BALANCE

Our base-case model assumes that current policies are maintained, primarily by holding the number of employees in the sector constant as a percentage of population, assuming state and local workers receive pay increases equal to those of private-sector employees, and assuming the total cost of many goods procured by the sector to provide services rises with increases in the population being served and the rate of inflation in the economy. We also developed an alternative scenario that calculates how much the sector would have to limit expenditures in the aggregate in order to avoid a negative operating balance. Figure 5 shows these two expenditure paths.

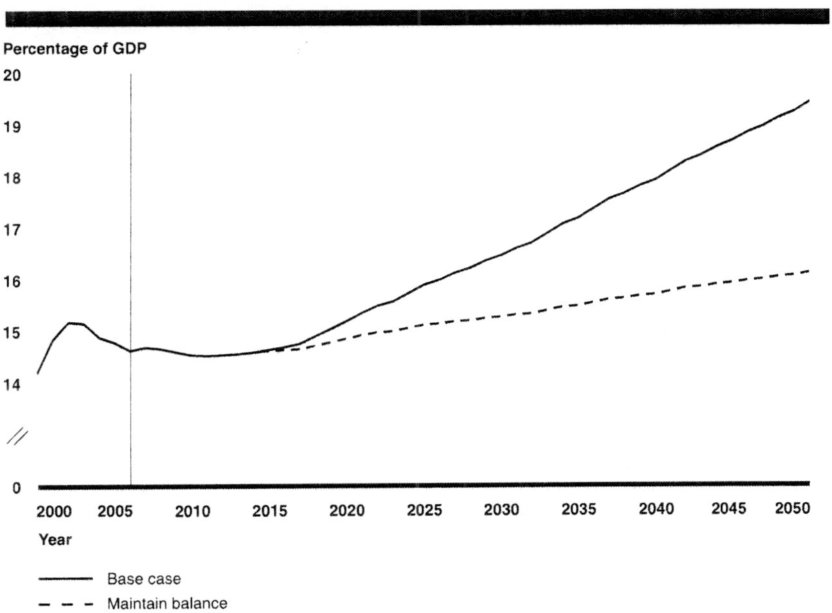

Sources: Historical data from NIPA and GAO analysis.

Note: Historical data are from 2000–2006. Projections are from 2007–2050.

Figure 5. Alternative Growth Scenarios: State and Local Expenditures, as a.

Figure 5 shows that under the base case, expenditures rise considerably over the simulation time frame. In contrast, maintaining balance solely through spending restraint would require holding expenditure growth to a much lower rate than the base case. Since a large percentage of expenditures of the sector are related to compensation of employees, this would likely mean that the workforce would not be able to grow as fast as we allow it to under the base case. That is, the ratio of employees to the population would need to decline. These state and local governments would also likely need to reduce their purchases of other goods and services procured to provide government services relative to what would have occurred under the base case. Since the base case was designed to reflect current policies, the results of the maintain balance scenario imply that there would need to be substantial cuts in expenditures and therefore services to citizens, relative to the base case.

Health Care Cost Growth Would Need to Be Held to Low Level to Prevent Declines in Fiscal Balances For the base-case model, we assumed that Medicaid expenditures grow according to CBO's intermediate projections—1 percentage point more than the growth in GDP per capita—and that employee and retiree health insurance expenditures grow over the next 30 years by an average of 1.4 percentage points more than GDP per capita and slowing to 0.6 percentage points by 2050. Given the importance of health care expenditures as a driver for the long-term fiscal outlook, we also model the impact of different health care expenditure growth assumptions. For a more optimistic scenario, we lowered Medicaid expenditure growth to CBO's lower spending path assumption. Under this path, Medicaid expenditure growth would equal the growth in GDP per capita. We also assumed no "excess cost growth" for the rate of increase in expenditures on employee and retiree health insurance, meaning that we hold the growth in these expenditures to the rate of growth in GDP per capita. For a more pessimistic scenario, we used CBO's high spending path assumption for Medicaid, under which costs rise at GDP plus 2.5 percent per capita, and we doubled the per capita rate of growth above GDP for health insurance expenditures.

Figure 6 shows the projected operating balance under all three health care cost-growth scenarios. The differences among the outcomes of these scenarios highlight the importance of health care to the long-term fiscal balance of the sector. With more rapidly rising health care expenditures, the operating balance falls off considerably more quickly than in the base case. Conversely, holding the growth in health care costs per capita to the overall per capita economic growth enables the sector to avert deficits during the projection time frame. Neither historical experience nor expert opinion, however, suggests that the cost growth of health care will likely be held to the level embodied in this optimistic scenario in the near future.

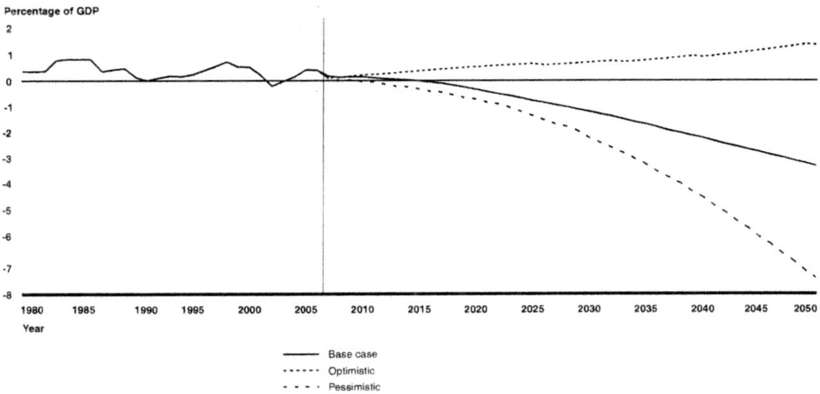

Sources: Historical data from NIPA and GAO analysis.

Note: Historical data are from 2000–2006. Projections are from 2007–2050. Optimistic Scenario Assumptions: State and local employee and retiree per capita health benefits grow at the same rate as per capita GDP, while other health expenditures grow according to CBO's low cost scenario. Pessimistic Scenario Assumptions: State and local employee and retiree per capita health benefits grow at the rate consistent with per capita GDP plus twice the excess cost factor, while other health expenditures grow according to CBO's high cost scenario.

Figure 6: Operating Balance Net of Funds for Capital Expenditures, Base Case and Alternative Cases Based on Health Care Costs.

Chapter 5

State and Local Fiscal Challenges Add to the Nation's Fiscal Difficulties

Since 1992, we have produced long-term simulations of what might happen to federal deficits and debt under various policy scenarios. Our most recent long-term federal simulations show ever-larger deficits resulting in a very large and growing federal debt burden over time. Just as in the state and local government sector, the federal fiscal difficulties stem primarily from an expected explosion of health-related expenditures. As we have noted elsewhere, the expected continued rise in health care costs poses a fiscal challenge not just to government budgets, but to American business and society as a whole. The fundamental fiscal problems of the federal government and these subnational governments are similar and are linked. Figure 7 shows two simulations for the federal fiscal path under alternative assumptions, and overlays the simulated fiscal imbalance of the state and local government sector.[15]

For the federal fiscal simulation denoted "baseline extended," we follow CBO baseline projections for the next 10 years: tax provisions that are scheduled to expire are assumed to do so and discretionary spending is assumed to grow with inflation. After the first 10 years, we use the Social Security and Medicare Trustees' 75-year intermediate ("best") estimates for those programs and CBO's midrange Medicaid estimates. All other expenditures and receipts are held constant as a share of GDP after the first 10 years. Under the alternative federal simulation, we assume that during the first 10 years of the simulation, expiring tax provisions are extended and that discretionary spending grows with GDP—a faster pace than inflation. After the 10-year time frame, we assume that action is taken to return and keep revenue at its historical share of GDP plus an additional amount attributable to deferred taxes (i.e., taxes on withdrawals from retirement accounts). This alternative also incorporates somewhat higher Medicare estimates reflecting a more realistic scenario for physician payments. The overlay of the base case state and local simulation shows that the state and local fiscal situation imposes further burden on the nation's economy in the next several decades.

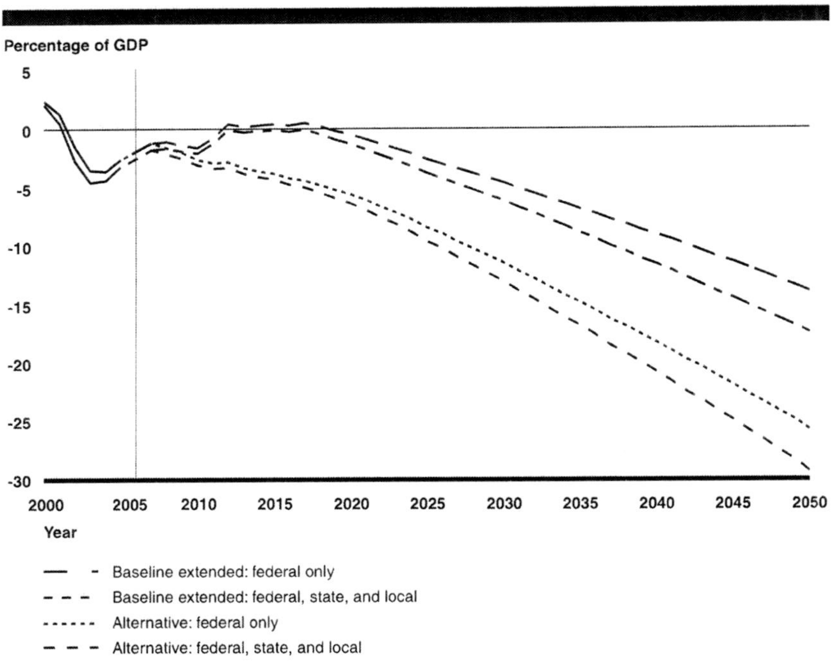

Sources: Historical data from NIPA and GAO analysis.

Note: Historical data are from 2000-2006. Projections are from 2007- 2050. The state and local balance measure is similar to the federal unified budget measure.

Figure 7. Federal and State and Local Surpluses and Deficits, as a Percentage of GDP.

We did our work from September 2007 through December 2007 in accordance with generally accepted government auditing standards. We provided a draft of this report to the Bureau of Economic Analysis of the Department of Commerce for technical review.

Appendix I

STATE AND LOCAL FISCAL MODEL METHODOLOGY

This appendix describes our simulations of state and local fiscal conditions. As an organizing framework and basic data source, the state and local government model relies on the National Income and Product Accounts (NIPA), prepared by the U.S. Department of Commerce. Table 3.3, State and Local Government Current Receipts and Expenditures, of the NIPA provides data on receipts and expenditures of all state and local governments in aggregate. We also use tables underlying table 3.3 to obtain more detailed information for some of the expenditure classifications. We project the growth in each category of receipts and expenditures using the Congressional Budget Office's (CBO) economic assumptions whenever possible. In several cases we were not able to obtain existing projections and needed to develop our own assumptions about the likely future growth path of certain receipts or expenditures. We also developed detailed models to project items such as necessary pension fund contributions, the costs of health insurance for employees and retirees, and several tax receipt categories. Our base-case model assumes current policies remain in place. Throughout this appendix we describe how that basic assumption is realized.

Once all receipts and expenditures of the sector are simulated forward through 2050, we develop summary indicators of the state and local government sector's fiscal status. Because the model covers the state and local government sector in the aggregate, the fiscal outcome of individual states and localities cannot be captured. Also, the model does not identify whether it is the state or the local government sector that faces greater fiscal challenges. The remainder of this appendix describes (1) how each of the receipt categories is projected; (2) how each of the expenditure categories is projected (with the exception of required pension contributions and the costs of health care, which are discussed more fully in app. III); and (3) how we develop measures of fiscal balance.

PROJECTION OF RECEIPTS OF THE STATE AND LOCAL GOVERNMENT SECTOR

The model provides projections for each type of receipt of state and local governments. The Bureau of Economic Analysis of the Department of Commerce assembles the NIPA based on data from the quinquennial Census of Governments, annual surveys of Government Finances, and other sources. In the NIPA, receipts are divided into five major categories: tax receipts, contributions for government social insurance, income receipts on assets, transfer receipts, and the current surplus of government enterprises. Figure 8 shows these categories as well as the breakdown of receipts within each of these classifications.

Tax Receipts

As noted in Figure 8 below, our base-case simulation is based on current policy and does not project any possible policy changes that would affect receipts during the simulation period. In the case of taxes, this means that we simulate the receipts that would be collected if tax rates and structures were to remain unchanged. Accordingly, several tax receipt categories grow at the same rate as their underlying tax bases. For several tax categories, however, it is more appropriate to project tax receipts themselves instead of their tax bases. Our tax receipt projections are based on a set of economic assumptions, many of which come from CBO.[16] However, most of CBO's projections extend only 10 years into the future. In order to project beyond 10 years, therefore, we used GDP values from GAO's long-term federal budget simulations in conjunction with extrapolations of CBO's economic assumptions.

1. Taxes:
- Personal income tax (state personal income tax and local personal income tax)
- Sales tax (general sales tax and selective [excise] sales tax)
- Corporate income tax
- Property tax
- Other taxes on production
- Estate tax

2. Contributions to government insurance

3. Income on financial assets owned by state and local governments

4. Transfer receipts:
- Federal Medicaid grants
- Non-Medicaid federal grants
- Federal investment grants (long-term investments such as roads, bridges, and other infrastructure)
- Transfers from businesses and persons (e.g., fines, tobacco settlements)

5. Surplus or deficit on government enterprises (e.g., liquor stores, public power, public transit, public housing)

Source: GAO organization of NIPA classifications.

Note: Unlike the NIPA, we do not distinguish between current and noncurrent receipts.

Figure 8. Receipt Classifications of State and Local Governments.

Personal Income Tax Receipts

Some states have progressive rate structures resulting in receipts growing faster than incomes. Because of this, for state income tax receipts, our modeling reflects this progressivity as we project receipts themselves rather than assume that receipts grow at the same rate as the tax base. As such, we simulate future state personal income tax receipts by estimating the long-run responsiveness, or elasticity, of receipts to taxable personal income.[17] The long-run elasticity estimate depicts the extent to which tax receipts grow in response to income growth but does not capture their short-run reaction to changes in income over the business cycle.[18]

We adjusted the historical state income tax receipt data to remove the effects of both policy changes as well as unusual capital gains that influenced past receipts. It is necessary to purge past data of policy changes because these can substantially influence the estimated elasticity, and including those effects would not maintain the "policy neutral" paradigm of our base case. Similarly, unusual swings in capital gains represent past events that may have had a significant impact on receipts but are not expected to recur in any predictable way. To purge the effect of policy changes from the receipts data, we used data from *The Fiscal Survey of the States:* December 2006, National Association of State Budget Officers (NASBO). These data provide estimates of the aggregate effect of tax changes each year. To remove the effect of atypical capital gains realizations on receipts, we estimated a relationship between the share of federal income tax receipts from capital gains receipts and the highest marginal tax rate on capital gains. Any deviation between the actual share of capital gains receipts and the share implied by this relationship was removed from state personal income taxes. Using the adjusted receipts data, we estimated that a 1 percent increase in real taxable personal income generates an approximate 1.1 percent increase in real personal income tax receipts. The somewhat greater growth in receipts than in income reflects the progressivity exhibited in some state income tax rate structures.

To project state personal income taxes in future years using this relationship, future values of taxable personal income are required. Ten-year taxable income projections come from CBO. Thereafter, taxable income is held constant as a share of GDP at CBO's projected tenth-year level. The estimated long-run elasticity of approximately 1.1 therefore implies that state personal income taxes increase slightly as a share of the economy over the projection period.

See appendix IV equation 34 for more information on the state income tax analysis.

In contrast to state personal income taxes, local personal income taxes as well as other personal taxes have displayed no discernable trend as a share of taxable personal income over the last 2 decades. In the base-case projections, therefore, we simply let these personal taxes grow at the same rate as taxable personal income. This implies that the local income and other personal tax rates remain unchanged over the simulation period. Because we allow these personal tax receipts to grow with taxable income and taxable income grows with GDP, local income and other personal taxes remain constant as a share of the economy in our long-term projections.

See appendix IV equations 35 and 36 for more information on the local income tax and other personal tax analysis.

Sales Tax Receipts

The model divides sales tax receipts into two categories, general and selective (or excise) sales taxes. General sales taxes are levied as a percentage of the price of the items purchased. In contrast, selective sales taxes—which are levied on such goods as liquor, gasoline, and tobacco—are often exacted in terms of dollars and/or cents per item purchased, and the amount of the tax may be adjusted only intermittently. Accordingly, the model uses different relationships for the two types of sales taxes.

General Sales Tax Receipts

In the absence of policy changes, general sales tax receipts should grow at the same rate as the consumption categories subject to the tax—that is, to the sales tax base. To evaluate the outlook for state and local government general sales tax receipts, we estimated the long-term responsiveness of our measure of the sales tax base to aggregate wage and salary income. Given projections of aggregate income, this elasticity provides a future path for the sales tax base. Receipts are then assumed to grow at the same rate as the tax base, implying that the average sales tax rate remains constant over the simulation period.

The first step in this analysis is to develop a broad consumption measure as a proxy for the tax base using previous work as a guide.[19] The proxy used here is total consumption expenditures excluding food and services, because the two categories are often not part of the sales tax base. In addition, because the sales tax base has been negatively affected by increases in mail order and Internet purchases, we also used Census data to remove an estimate of remote sales from the tax base. We then estimated the long-run elasticity of this sales tax base with respect to aggregate wages and salaries using historical data. We found that the estimated elasticity is 0.93, suggesting that over the long run, a 1.0 percent increase in real wages and salaries results in a 0.93 percent increase in the real sales tax base. In the projections, sales tax receipts grow at the same rate as the sales tax base. The sluggish growth in sales tax receipts relative to the economy reflects the shift in consumer spending toward services and remote sales, both of which are excluded from our proxy for the sales tax base.

To accommodate the possible success of efforts to include remote sales in the tax base, we also estimated the long-run income elasticity of a sales tax base measure that includes remote sales. The resulting estimate of 0.97 implies that, even if remote sales were to be taxed, general sales tax receipts would still be unlikely to fully keep pace with overall economic growth.

See appendix IV equations 37, 38, 39, and 41 for more information on the general sales tax analysis

Selective Sales (Excise) Tax Receipts

In addition to the general sales tax, state and local governments impose a variety of selective sales (or excise) taxes on gasoline, alcoholic beverages, tobacco, public utilities, insurance receipts, and other items. Selective sales taxes generally take the form of a given amount of tax for each unit purchased, (i.e., a unit tax). Most states, for example, levy a tax on gasoline which takes the form of a certain number of cents per gallon. Because the amount of the unit tax is adjusted only periodically, selective sales tax receipts tend to grow less rapidly than the value of the sales on which they are levied and less than incomes. Accordingly, we estimated the responsiveness of selective sales tax receipts to income rather than the responsiveness of the tax base to income. Our estimates indicated that the long-run elasticity, based on historic data, was 0.80. This implies that these receipts tend to grow much less than income and the general economy.

See appendix IV equation 43 for more information on the selective sales (excise) tax analysis.

Taxes on Corporate Income

In our simulations, corporate tax receipts grow at the same rate as CBO's projections of corporate profits. After an initial adjustment period, CBO assumes profits will keep pace with overall economic growth. In our long-run simulations, therefore, corporate income taxes remain constant as a share of the economy.

See appendix IV equation 49 for more information on the corporate income tax analysis.

Property Tax Receipts

Property tax receipts are assumed to grow with our projections of the property tax base. In turn, property tax base projections are based on our estimate of the relationship between real GDP and the real market value of real estate owned by both the household sector and the nonfarm, nonfinancial business sector. Data for the market value of real estate are obtained from the sectors' balance sheets in the Federal Reserve Board's flow of funds accounts. We estimated that the long-run responsiveness of property values to GDP is 1.13, which implies that the property tax base tends to grow somewhat more than GDP.

See appendix IV equations 44, 45, 46, and 47 for more information on the property tax analysis.

Other Taxes on Production

States and localities also collect a variety of other taxes, fees, and assessments that are classified in the NIPA as "other taxes on production." These include such items as motor vehicle license fees, severance taxes, and special assessments. In our projections, we assume these receipts grow at the same rate as GDP.

See appendix IV equation 48 for more information on the analysis of other taxes on production.

Estate and Gift Taxes

In the NIPA, estate and gift taxes are considered capital transfer receipts rather than current tax receipts. This distinction has some relevance for how fiscal balance measures are calculated, as discussed later in this appendix. In the projections, we assume that taxes on estates and gifts grow at a rate equal to the yield on 10-year Treasury securities.

See appendix IV equation 90 for more information on the estate and gift tax analysis.

Contributions for Government Social Insurance

Contributions for government social insurance are a small component of state and local governments' total current receipts related to payments for items such as disability insurance and unemployment coverage. The model assumes these tax receipts grow at the same rate as total wage and salary disbursements in the economy.

See appendix IV equation 50 for more information on the analysis of contributions for government social insurance.

Income Receipts on Assets

Income receipts on assets include interest receipts, dividends, and rents and royalties earned on the financial holdings of state and local governments. Projections of income receipts on assets require future values for both the effective rate earned on financial assets and total financial assets owned by the sector. These calculations are discussed in appendix II.

Current Transfer Receipts

Current transfer receipts include several major categories of state and local government nontax receipts. These include three types of federal grants-in-aid: federal Medicaid grants, other federal grants for current expenditures, and federal investment grants. The sector also receives transfers from business and persons, such as fines and tobacco settlement payments.

Federal Medicaid Grants

To project federal Medicaid grants in our base case, the model uses CBO's intermediate growth Medicaid outlay projections. For the first 10 years these are available in the most recent edition of CBO's Budget and Economic Outlook.[20] Thereafter, we use CBO's projections for Medicaid outlays as a share of GDP from the most recent long-term budget publication.[21]

Following the NIPA treatment, we subtract the "clawback" from Medicaid grants. Because of the passage of Medicare Part D, states pay the federal government a portion of the costs of prescription drugs previously covered under the Medicaid program. Thus, the Medicare Part D program will save states some of the payments they would have made towards prescription drugs under Medicaid to enrollees. The returned portion that states are required to remit is known as the clawback. CBO has estimated the clawback for the first 10 years. Thereafter, we extrapolate the clawback as a constant percentage of total federal Medicaid grants in the tenth year of CBO's estimates.

See appendix IV equations 54 and 55 for more information on the analysis of federal Medicaid grants.

Other Federal Grants to Finance Current Expenditures

In addition to Medicaid grants, the federal government provides grants intended to finance other current expenditures of state and local governments. Examples include grants for education, welfare and social services, and housing and community services. For the first 10 years, we project other federal grants for current spending by subtracting CBO's Medicaid grant projections from CBO's projection of total grants for current expenditures. After the first 10 years, we assume that other current grants grow with inflation plus population growth, keeping the real grant level per person stable, which is our implementation of a current policy scenario.

Federal Investment Grants

Because federal investment grants finance investment, rather than current expenditures, the NIPA classifies investment grants as a form of capital transfer. While capital transfers are not part of the state and local government sector's current receipts, they are included in the sector's total receipts. For the first 10 years of the projections, we assume that federal investment grants grow at the same rate as CBO's projections for federal capital transfers. After the first 10 years, we assume that investment grants grow with inflation plus population growth, which again reflects our implementation of a current policy scenario.

Transfers from Business and Persons

Transfers from business include state and local fines and other nontaxes, such as tobacco settlements. Similarly, personal transfer payments to government include donations, fees, and fines. Both types of private transfers are assumed to grow with GDP in the projections.

See appendix IV equations 56 and 57 for more information on the analysis of transfers from businesses and persons.

Current Surplus or Deficit of Government Enterprises

The current surplus or deficit of government enterprises is the difference between receipts and costs for a variety of businesslike operations of state and local governments. These enterprises provide such services as water, sewerage, gas, electricity, toll facilities, liquor stores, air and water terminals, housing and urban renewal, public transit, and a residual category covering such items as lotteries. As we examined the trends in the various enterprises we found that some types of enterprises tend to have surpluses (e.g., lotteries, liquor stores), some tend to have deficits (e.g., public transit, public housing), and some tend to run roughly at a break-even level (e.g., electricity, water). The overall balance for the entire state and local enterprise sector was sometimes positive and sometimes negative. We determined that no trend could be established and we therefore assumed that across all state and local governments and across all the types of enterprises, the budgets are balanced. We therefore set the balance for the enterprise sector equal to zero.

See appendix IV equation 58 for more information on the analysis of the current surplus or deficit of government enterprises.

PROJECTION OF EXPENDITURES OF THE STATE AND LOCAL GOVERNMENT SECTOR

In the NIPA, expenditures are divided into five categories, some much larger than others. Figure 9 shows the five types. Consumption expenditures, the largest category, includes such items as the compensation of state and local government employees. Transfer payments include Medicaid payments. Smaller classifications are: interest paid on the outstanding debt of these governments, subsidies, and expenditures for investments in fixed capital and nonproduced assets.

1. Consumption expenditures
   - Compensation of employees
     - Wages and salaries
     - Pension fund contributions
     - Heath care payments
     - Other employee benefits (e.g., life insurance)
   - Consumption of fixed capital (i.e., depreciation)
   - Miscellaneous consumption expenditures
     - Purchases of intermediate goods
     - Offsets related to tuition, hospitals, and certain other services not considered enterprises
     - Own account investments–offsets related to expenditures classified as consumption expenditures in the given year but really related to longer-term investments

2. Transfer payments to citizens
   - Medicaid and other health payments
   - Non-Medicaid transfers

3. Interest paid on outstanding state and local debt

4. Subsidies

5. Purchases of fixed assets and purchases of non-produced assets (mostly land)

Source: GAO organization of NIPA classifications.

Figure 9. Expenditure Classifications of State and Local Governments.

Consumption Expenditures

Consumption expenditures include an array of expenses related to direct spending to finance current operations. The largest component of these expenses is compensation of state and local government workers. In addition, the implicit cost of depleted capital—or depreciation—is a consumption expenditure. Other consumption expenditures include intermediate goods and services used to provide current services. Certain offsets are also made against consumption expenditures in the form of receipts for services the sector provides and the costs of investment goods the sector itself produces.

Compensation of State and Local Government Employees

The model projects several categories of employee compensation. These include (1) wages and salaries, (2) pension plan contributions, (3) employee and retiree health care costs, and (4) other employee benefits.

Wages and Salaries

In our base-case projections, which hold policy constant, we let employment grow with the population projections in the 2007 Social Security Trustees' report and allowed wages and salaries per employee to grow with CBO's projected increase in the employment cost index for private sector wages and salaries. These assumptions permit the sector to keep the number of employees per citizen constant while paying salaries that keep pace with those in the private sector. These assumptions reflect our judgment about how to implement a current policy scenario for these factors.

See appendix IV equation 9 for more information on the projections of wages and salaries.

Pension Plan Contributions

The model includes a set of relationships that solve for the contribution that state and local sector employers must make in order to fund pension plans on an ongoing basis. These relationships are explained in appendix III.

Health Insurance Contributions

We developed estimates of the aggregate cost to state and local governments for the health insurance of both active and retired employees.

These costs are projected on a pay-as-you-go basis and their derivation is described in appendix III.

Other Employee Benefits

Other employee benefits include life insurance and workers compensation contributions. These expenditures are assumed to grow with employment in the sector plus increases in the employee cost index for wages and salaries.

See appendix IV equation 68 for more information on the projections of other employee benefits.

Consumption of Fixed Capital (Depreciation)

Consumption of fixed capital, or depreciation, is another component of NIPA state and local government consumption. We calculated depreciation in a given year as a constant percentage of the prior year's capital stock.

Thus, the projections of investment, depreciation, and the capital stock are all interrelated. From a starting point for the level of capital stock in 2006, we increase the level of capital going forward each year by an estimate of gross investment. We assume that gross investment grows with population growth and inflation—our implementation of a current policy scenario. We then subtract a portion of the previous year's capital stock to reflect depreciation. The depreciation rate used in the projections is 2.8 percent, which is based on values for real consumption of fixed capital relative to real capital stock reported in recent years of NIPA data.

See appendix IV equations 70 through 75 for more information on the projections of the consumption of fixed capital (depreciation).

Miscellaneous Consumption Expenditures

The final component of consumption expenditures is a miscellaneous category that is equal to other consumptions expenditures minus two items: own-account investment and sales to other services.

1. Other consumption expenditures include such intermediate purchases as rent, gasoline, utilities, and supplies.

2. Own-account investment is the compensation of employees and the expenditures related to the sector's own production of investment goods, such as software and other capital assets. Because own-account investment expenditures represent the acquisition of long-term assets and are included in purchases of fixed assets, they must be subtracted from consumption expenditures to avoid double counting these expenses.
3. Sales to other sectors include tuition and related educational charges, health and hospital charges, and other sales of goods and services sold by the state and local sector that are not considered enterprise sales. Since these revenues are derived from the provision of services funded by consumption expenditures, they are netted against the costs of providing those services.

Despite the three separable components contained within this final classification of consumption expenditures, the model does not include explicit relationships explaining each of these components. Instead, we assume that other consumption will grow with inflation plus population growth.

See appendix IV equation 69 for more information on the projections of miscellaneous consumption expenditures.

Transfer Payments to Persons

The model divides state and local government transfer payments to persons into two categories, medical care payments and other transfers to persons. Medical care transfers include both Medicaid and other medical care payments, the latter of which consist of general medical assistance and the state children's health insurance program (SCHIP). The other transfer category includes a broad array of payments to individuals such as workers' compensation, temporary disability, and family assistance.

Medical Care Transfer Payments

Because the Medicaid program provides matching grants to state governments, Medicaid grants and medical care transfer payments generally have been closely related. The close relationship between Medicaid grants and transfer payments supports modeling medical care transfers as a constant multiple of CBO's projection for Medicaid grants. In recent years, the ratio of the sector's medical transfer payments to Medicaid grants was 1.726, which implies that the federal government ultimately paid about 58 percent of total state and local medical care payments (including Medicaid, general medical assistance, and SCHIP payments) while states financed 42 percent of the total with their own funds. This relationship is applied to CBO's Medicaid grant projections—which are available to 2050—for our projections of state and local medical care payments.

See appendix IV equation 77 for more information on the projections of medical care transfer payments.

Nonmedical Transfer Payments to Persons

Nonmedical transfer payments include a broad array of transfers such as temporary disability insurance, workers' compensation, family assistance, education assistance, foster care, adoption assistance, and expenditures for food under the supplemental program for Women, Infants, and Children. In our base-case projections of these payments, real spending per capita is kept constant, reflecting our current policy scenario. Equivalently, payments grow with inflation and population growth.

See appendix IV equation 78 for more information on the projections of nonmedical transfer payments to persons.

Interest Paid

State and local governments pay interest on their outstanding debt. Interest payment projections require estimates of future effective interest rates on debt and the amount of debt outstanding. This discussion requires more detail and is explained in appendix II.

Subsidies

Subsidies are a very small remaining category of current expenditures consisting mainly of payments to railroads. California's payments to electricity suppliers from 2001 through 2003 were also classified as subsidies. In the simulations, subsidies are assumed to grow with inflation and population.

See appendix IV equation 84 for more information on the projections of subsidies.

Gross Investment and Purchases of Nonproduced Assets

Because they are capital outlays, gross investment and purchases of nonproduced assets are considered to be investment expenditures. As such they are not considered a current expenditure. Investment expenditures cover the acquisition of all longer-lived assets including structures, equipment, and software, and nonproduced assets consist of the net acquisition of land less oil bonuses. We grow both of these factors at the combined rate of inflation and population growth.

See appendix IV equations 70, 71, and 92 for more information on the projections of gross investment and the purchase of nonproduced assets.

MEASURES OF FISCAL BALANCE

We use two measures of fiscal balance in our report: net lending or borrowing and the operating balance. In addition, a third measure—net saving—is not directly discussed but is a conceptually important measure.

Net Lending or Borrowing

The first projected balance measure is NIPA's net lending or borrowing, which is the difference between total receipts and total expenditures and is analogous to the federal unified surplus or deficit. Thus, this balance is measured as the sum of all receipts discussed in this appendix minus all expenditures, with one exception. While the measure of total expenditures used to calculate net lending or borrowing includes both current expenditures and capital expenditures, it excludes the consumption of fixed capital (depreciation) because the latter is not a cash outlay. The value of net lending or borrowing must be financed by some combination of changes in financial assets and liabilities.

See appendix IV equation 93 for more information on measurement of net lending or borrowing.

Operating Balance Net of Funds for Capital Expenditures

The second balance measure we use is a GAO-developed measure that we call the operating balance excluding funds for capital expenditures. This measure is designed to be roughly akin to the operating budgets of subnational governments—budgets which these governments are generally required to balance or nearly balance. We develop a measure of receipts not available to finance current spending as the difference between investment spending and the change in medium- and long-term debt. Subtracting this amount from total receipts leaves the estimated receipts that are available to finance current expenditures. The expenditure component of the balance measure excludes both investment spending and depreciation.

Our operating balance measure includes two further adjustments to NIPA-based totals. First, we exclude the current surplus/deficit of government enterprises from receipts because state and local government operating budgets exclude government enterprises. This adjustment has no effect on our base case simulations because we assume the balance is equal to zero, but its incorporation accommodates potential alternative assumptions about the current balance of government enterprises. We also exclude a category of funds that we call the net balance of social insurance funds. As noted earlier, state and local employees as well as employers make contributions to social insurance funds to pay for such items as temporary disability and workers' compensation insurance. Although not explicitly mentioned earlier, payments from these funds are embedded in transfer payments that governments pay to workers when they are disabled or otherwise entitled to payments from these insurance funds. In our simulations, the balance is assumed to grow with total wage and salary disbursements. While governments hold balances in these funds, the funds are not available for operating expenses.

See appendix IV equation 94 for more information on the measurement of the operating balance net of funds for capital expenditures.

Net State and Local Government Saving

The model also solves for net state and local government saving, which is a key balance measure in the NIPA that has important macroeconomic implications. Net state and local government saving is simply the sum of all current receipts (that is, all receipts discussed earlier except investment grants and estate taxes) minus the sum of all current expenditures, where current expenditures include the consumption of fixed capital (depreciation) but exclude investment spending.

See appendix IV equation 85 for more information on the measurement of net saving.

Appendix II

Projections of Income Earned on Assets and Interest Paid on Liabilities of the State and Local Sector

This appendix describes how we developed estimates of financial earnings and interest paid on outstanding debt for the state and local government sector. This analysis starts with a method for translating state and local government budget surpluses or deficits—as measured by the difference between its total receipts and expenditures and labeled net lending or borrowing—into changes in the sector's financial assets and financial liabilities. We also describe how we estimated the effective rate earned on the sector's financial assets and the effective rate paid on its credit market liabilities in each year and applied these rates to the prior year's assets and liabilities, respectively, to provide estimates of the sector's asset income and interest payments.

Budget Outcomes and Financial Assets and Liabilities

For any entity, there is a direct relationship between budget outcomes and changes in financial position. In particular, if expenditures exceed receipts, the gap needs to be financed by some combination of changes in financial assets and changes in financial liabilities—that is, if governments spend more than they take in, they must pay for it by issuing debt, cashing in assets, or some combination of the two. Conversely, if receipts exceed expenditures and the sector is a net lender, its net financial investment (the net change in financial assets minus the net change in financial liabilities) must equal the budget surplus. The relationship between budget outcomes and the sector's financial position is shown in the following accounting identity:

total receipts - total expenditures = change in financial assets - change in financial liabilities

For a given difference between total receipts and total expenditures, that is, the value of net lending or borrowing, various combinations of changes in financial assets and changes in financial liabilities can satisfy this identity. To leverage this relationship for our projections we use two methods. The first applies when net lending or borrowing is in its historical range. The second is necessary for a good portion of our simulations because the ever-growing deficits that we find are inconsistent with historical experience, and relying on the first method would produce unrealistic results.

Method Used When Budget Outcomes Are in Historical Range

Traditionally, total expenditures have usually exceeded total receipts, and the sector has been a net borrower. But the gap has rarely been large, so the borrowing requirements have usually been modest. If our estimate of net lending or borrowing falls into a range similar to historical experience, we invoke the accounting identity above by estimating the growth in four components of financial liabilities of the sector as provided in the Federal Reserve's Flow of Funds Accounts. These components include three types of credit market instruments: short-term municipal securities, medium- and long-term municipal securities, and U.S. government loans, as well as "trade payables," which are related to the acquisition of goods and services for conducting operations, and are not credit market liabilities.[1] The growth in the values of these four types of liabilities, along with the estimate of net lending or borrowing, then determines the change in assets necessary to satisfy the identity. When the size of the balances is consistent with historical experience, the model projects each of these financial liabilities as follows:

- Short-term debt. The model includes an econometric equation linking short-term debt to net saving. The equation also includes several dummy variables controlling for periods of unusual changes in short-term debt, and autoregressive and moving average error terms to control for serial correlation of the residuals and improve the equation's fit. The equation indicates that short-term debt issuance is inversely related to the sector's net saving, which implies that past deficits were financed in part by short-term borrowing.
- Medium- and long-term debt. Changes in medium- and long-term municipal debt are mostly linked to capital expenditures (including land) and their financing. Some combination of tax receipts, federal investment grants, and debt can be used to finance state and local government investment. Accordingly, a relationship was estimated in which the change in the municipal bond rate explains how much debt is used to finance the gap between investment spending and federal investment grants. The equation also includes dummy variables covering periods when tax considerations and other unusual factors had an important role in the amount of debt issued. These dummy variables control for unusually large long-term debt issuances in 1978 and 1985 and unusually large decreases in outstanding long-term debt in 1994 and 1995. The projections assume that similar events will not occur over the simulation period. The relationship also includes an autoregressive term to control for the serial correlation of the error term.
- Borrowing from the U.S. Treasury. The state and local government sector also borrows modest amounts from the U.S. Treasury. Our estimates imply that real growth in borrowing from the Treasury is negatively affected by real GDP growth. During periods of relatively strong growth, the sector borrowed less from the Treasury and during periods of slow or negative growth, the sector borrowed more. The estimated equation also includes dummy variables to control for unusual borrowing increases in 1984 and 1985 and an unusual decrease in borrowing in 1988, along with autoregressive and moving average error terms.
- Trade payables. Trade payables help finance the goods and services the sector acquires in the conduct of its operations. Accordingly, our base-case simulations let trade payables grow at the same rate as other consumption expenditures, which, in turn, grow with inflation plus population growth.

As noted above, the historical tendency has been for the state and local government sector to run small deficits and an occasional surplus as measured by net lending or borrowing. The method we have described documents how we use the accounting identity to grow financial assets and liabilities in similar circumstances. If the sector runs large deficits, however, as we find within a few years of our simulation, this methodology generates unrealistic financial outcomes. In particular, if the method were used throughout our simulation analysis, ever-increasing deficits would lead to declining values of financial assets—because under this method, assets are the residual variable that balances the accounting identity. In later years assets would decline so substantially that they would become negative. Since this makes no economic sense because governments require funds to meet current expenses, we developed an alternative method that is triggered when key relationships become out of balance in our simulation.

Alternative Method for Determining Changes in Financial Assets and Liabilities

Our methodology "switch" is triggered when receipts fall so substantially short of expenditures—i.e., the sector is a substantial net borrower—that assets grow less than gross domestic product (GDP). If this occurs, in the next period the model changes how short-term debt is projected. Rather than being independently projected, short-term debt then becomes the residual variable that satisfies the accounting identity. In this alternative case, assets grow with GDP.

Projecting Income Receipts on Assets and Interest Payments on Debt

Income receipts on assets are part of the sector's receipts while its interest payments are part of its expenditures. We have described how the model determines the change in assets and liabilities in each year. These earnings or payments are calculated by setting an appropriate rate and applying that rate to these asset or liability values, respectively. In this section we describe how we determine the effective rates earned and paid and how we use those rates and the values of assets and liabilities to project asset income and interest payments of the state and local sector.

Income Receipts on Financial Assets

Income receipts on assets are reported as a category of receipts in the National Income and Product Accounts (NIPA). We divide the income receipts on assets by the value of financial assets at the end of the previous year to calculate historical values for the effective rate earned on assets in each past year. The evolution of these past effective rates reflects the turnover of old assets and the acquisition of new financial assets by state and local governments. This process can be captured by setting the effective rate earned on assets in a given year equal to a weighted average of the prior period's effective rate and the given year's prevailing market rate on the types of assets that the sector purchases.

Using a simple regression model we developed weights of 0.81 for the prior year's effective rate earned and 0.19 for the given year's yield on 3-month Treasury securities, projections of which are available from the Congressional Budget Office (CBO). As stated, these weights reflect the gradual turnover and replacement of assets with newer issues. The product of the effective rate earned and the prior period's financial assets equals the income earned on assets.

Interest Paid on Credit Market Liabilities

A similar method is used to derive interest paid on outstanding debt of the sector. First, we divide the sector's interest paid by the value of credit market liabilities outstanding at the end of the previous year to calculate historical values for the effective rate paid on liabilities in each past year. To develop weights for the simulations, we then model the effective rate of interest paid as a weighted average of the effective return in the previous period and the Aaa municipal bond rate for the given year. Based on our analysis, we set the effective rate paid equal to 0.88 times the prior year's effective rate paid plus 0.12 times the given year's projected Aaa municipal bond yield. These weights reflect the gradual turnover and replacement of municipal securities with newer issues.

We generated our own projections of the municipal bond yield based on a relationship we estimated between the Moody's Aaa municipal bond yield and the 10-year Treasury yield. We then use the estimated relationship and CBO's projections of the 10-year Treasury yield to calculate future values of the municipal bond yield. The sector's interest payments are equal to the product of the effective interest rate paid and the sector's prior year liabilities excluding trade payables. In the model, therefore, explicit interest payments only apply to the sector's credit market liabilities.

Appendix III

Pension and Retiree Health Care Projections

This appendix provides information on the development of simulations of future pension and health care expenditures for retirees of state and local governments.[1] In particular, we provide information on (1) the development of several key demographic and economic factors such as future employment, retirement, and wages for the state and local workforce that are necessary for the simulations of future pension and retiree health care costs; (2) how we project the necessary contribution rate to pension funds of state and local governments; and (3) how we project the future yearly pay-as-you-go expenditures of employee and retiree health insurance.

Development of Factors for Employment, Retirement, Wages, and Benefits

Key underlying information for the pension and health care expenditure simulations relate to future levels of employment, retirees, and wages. In particular, to estimate the expenditures for the post-retirement promises the sector has and will continue to make as well as expenditures for health care for active employees, we need to project the number of employees and retirees in each future year, as well as the dollar value of pension benefits that will be earned and the extent to which those benefits will be funded through employee contributions to pension funds. The cost of health care and the estimate of employees and retirees receiving health care benefits are discussed later in this appendix. We project the following key factors for each year during the simulation time frame: (1) the number of state and local government employees, (2) state and local government real wages, (3) the number of pension beneficiaries, (4) average real benefits per beneficiary, and (5) yearly employee contributions to state and local government pension plans.

Steps to Project Future Employment Levels

To project the level of employment in each future year, we assume that state and local employment grows at the same rate as total population under the intermediate assumptions of the Board of Trustees of the Old Age, Survivors, and Disability Insurance (OASDI), commonly referred to as Social Security[2]—that is, we assume that the ratio of state and local employment to total population remains constant.[3] The Trustees assume that population growth gradually declines from 0.8 percent during the next decade to a steady rate of 0.3 percent per year beginning in 2044. Accordingly, state and local government employment growth displays the same pattern in our projections.

Steps to Project Future State and Local Government Real Wages

The pension benefits that employees become entitled to are a function of the wages they earned during their working years. We assume that the real employment cost index for the state and local sector will grow at a rate equal to the difference between the Congressional Budget Office (CBO) assumptions for the growth in the employment cost index (ECI) for private sector wages and salaries and inflation as measured by the consumer price index for all urban consumers.[4] CBO's assumptions for growth in the ECI and the Consumer Price Index for All Urban Consumers (CPI-U) are 3.3 percent and 2.2 percent per year, respectively, implying a real wage growth of 1.1 percent per year during the simulation time frame.

Aggregate real wages are assumed to grow at the combined rate of growth in the real employment cost index we have just described, and the level of employment. As noted previously, the Trustees project that population growth slows from 0.8 percent in the upcoming decade to a steady rate of 0.3 percent after 2044. Because population growth drives employment in our projections, this slowdown implies that aggregate real wage growth slows from 1.9 percent per year to a steady long-run rate of 1.4 percent.

Steps to Project Growth in the Number of Pension Beneficiaries

Future growth in the number of state and local government retirees—many of whom will be entitled to pension and health care benefits—is largely driven by the size of the workforce in earlier years. While actuaries use detailed information and assumptions regarding the age, earnings, service records, and mortality rates applicable to the entities they evaluate, information in such detail is not available for the state and local government sector as a whole. This lack of detailed data necessitated the development of a method of projecting aggregate state and local beneficiary growth that is much simpler than the methods that actuaries employ.

The method we developed reflects the logic that each year's growth in the number of beneficiaries is linked to past growth in the number of employees. Total state and local government employment from 1929 through 2005 was obtained from the national income and product accounts (NIPA) tables 6.4a, b, c, and d. The Census Bureau provided data on the number of state and local pension beneficiaries from 1992 through 2005 during which continuous observations were available. Cyclical swings in the employment series were removed using a Hodrick-Prescott filter. Then, both the employment and beneficiary series were logged and first-differenced, transforming the data from levels to proportionate changes. We developed a routine that searched across 45 years of lagged employment growth to select a set of weights for the years in which past employment growth best explained a given year's growth in beneficiaries.[5] The routine included the restrictions that the weights must be nonnegative and sum to one.

The method produced a relationship that reflected the contribution of a particular past year's employment change in explaining a given year's change in retirees. In particular, the estimated relationship suggests that beneficiary growth in a given year is largely determined by employment growth 21, 22, 23, and 34 years prior to the given period. This pattern appears consistent with the categories of workers that the sector employs. Many fire and police positions, for example, offer faster pension accrual or early retirement due to the physical demands and risks of the work, while many other state and local workers have longer careers.

Steps to Project Real Benefits Per Beneficiary

While, in the long run, the average real benefit level should grow at the same rate as real wages—that is, at 1.1 percent per year—in the first decades of the projection the average real benefit will be affected by real wage changes that occurred before the projection period. Accordingly, we developed a relationship that reflects how the average real benefit level will change over time according to changes in the number and average real benefit level of three subsets of the retiree population: (1) new retirees entering the beneficiary pool, (2) new decedents leaving the pool, and (3) the majority of the previous year's retirees who continue to receive benefits during the given period. Each group's real benefit is linked to the real wage level in the average year of retirement for that group. Thus, to determine the average real benefit overall in any future year, we need weights and real wage indexes for the three groups that can be used to develop a rolling average real wage of the recipient pool in each future year.

Earlier we described how we project the percentage change in the total number of beneficiaries between two successive years, but this difference is actually comprised of two elements: the percentage change in new retirees minus the percentage change in decedents. Therefore, to determine the weight for new retirees, we also need an estimate of the number of new decedents in each year. In order to estimate a "death rate," we utilize Social Security Administration data on terminated benefits[6] and total Social Security recipients, which excludes disability recipients.[7] Our death rate for the forecast period is set equal to the number of terminated Social Security recipients divided by the total number of Social Security recipients in 2003—3.67 percent.[8] This analysis then enables a derivation of weights for each of the three groups as follows:

- weight for new retirees: the number of beneficiaries this year, less the number of beneficiaries last year who are still alive, divided by the number of beneficiaries this year;
- weight for continuing recipients is equal to last year's beneficiaries divided by this year's beneficiaries; and
- weight for the deceased is the death rate multiplied by last year's beneficiaries divided by this year's beneficiaries.

Next, we identied the real employment cost index that determines the real benefit level for each of these three groups. We do so by estimating the average retirement year applicable to each of the three groups. First, we assume the average retirement age is 60. We developed this estimate based on an analysis of the March Supplement to the Current Population Survey (CPS) for 2005-2006, which indicated that the average state and local government retiree had retired at 60 years of age. We also analyzed detailed data on the age distribution of Social Security recipients provided by the Office of the Actuary of the Social Security Administration. These data showed that the average age for new decedents is about 81 during the initial years of OASDI's simulations, and we thus used a 21-year lag—81 minus 60—to estimate the real wage applicable to this group. For the newly retired group, we use the given year's employment cost index. For the remaining retirees—those already retired and remaining in the group—we use information from CPS for 2005 which indicated that the average age of a retired state or local retiree was 68. Therefore, we apply an 8-year lag to the real employment cost index to determine real benefits of this group. We then use this information to create a weighted average employment cost index for the retiree pool in any given year.

The ratio of the given year's weighted average real wage index to the previous year's weighted average real wage index should equal the ratio of the current to the previous year's average real benefit levels. Thus, a given year's average real benefit level grows at the same rate as the rolling index of real wages. The relationship has the desired property of capturing the effect of historical real wage growth in the initial decades of the projection before converging to a long-run average annual growth rate of 1.1 percent, which is consistent with our assumption for real wage growth. To calculate aggregate real pension benefit payments, the average real benefit is multiplied by the number of beneficiaries projected.

Steps to Project Employee Contributions to Pension Funds

Employee contributions represent an important funding source for state and local government pension plans. In 2006, for example, NIPA data indicate that employees contributed 4.5 percent of their wages and salaries to their retirement funds. To estimate future employee contributions, we simply assume that the 2006 contribution level is held constant as a share of aggregate wages.

PROJECTIONS OF NECESSARY CONTRIBUTIONS TO PENSION FUNDS FOR STATE AND LOCAL GOVERNMENT SECTOR

The purpose of the pension simulations is to estimate the steady contribution rate that state and local governments would need to make each year going forward to ensure that their pension systems are fully funded on an ongoing basis. Our goal is to estimate the financial commitments to employees that have been and are likely to continue to be made by the state and local sector to better understand the full fiscal outlook for the sector. As such, our analysis projects the liabilities that the sector is likely to continue to incur in the future.

In the previous section we discussed how we calculate a variety of critical demographic and economic factors that are necessary for this analysis. The necessary contribution rate can now be derived according to straightforward logic: the benefits that are promised to employees (including liabilities already made and promises that will be made in the future) must be paid from three sources: (1) existing pension fund assets at our starting point in 2006, (2) contributions that employees will continue to make to those funds in the future, and (3) contributions that employers will make to those funds in the future. Mathematically we start with the present value of future pension benefits. We then subtract two things: the value of pension fund financial assets in 2006—which was approximately $2.979 trillion[9]—and the present value of employee contributions. The present value of the remaining liability is the value that the governments must fund. We then divide that present value by the present value of future wages. This yields the steady level of employer contribution, relative to wages, that would need to be made in every year between 2006 and 2050 to fully fund promised pension benefits.

Although we are only interested in developing necessary contribution rates over the simulation time frame—that is, until 2050—we actually have to derive the contribution rate for a longer time frame in order to find the steady level of necessary contributions. This longer time frame is required because the estimated contribution rate increases as the projection horizon increases and eventually converges to a steady state. If the projection period is of insufficient length, the steady level of contribution is not attained and the necessary contribution rate is understated.[10] As such, all of the flows in the calculation extend 400 years into the future. We use a real rate of return on pension assets of 5.0 percent to discount future flows when deriving present values.[11]

Applying this analysis, we found that in aggregate, state and local government contributions to pension funds would need to increase by less than half a percent to fund, on an ongoing basis, the pension liabilities they have and will continue to incur. In particular, the 2006 pension contributions for the sector amounted to 9 percent of wages, and our base-case estimate is that the level would need to be 9.3 percent each year to fully fund pensions.

To examine the sensitivity of our model results we altered our assumptions regarding the expected real yield, and found that the model results are highly sensitive to this rate. For our primary simulations, we based the expected real yield on actual returns on various investment instruments over the last 40 years as well as the disposition of the portfolio of assets held by the sector over the last 10 years. This generated a real yield of 5 percent. But some pension experts have expressed concern that returns on equities in the future may not be quite as high as those in the past. In fact, some analysts believe that an analysis of this type should only consider "riskless returns." Under such an approach we would assume that all pension funds are invested in very safe financial instruments such as government bonds. We estimated the necessary steady level of employer contributions holding all elements in the model stable except the real expected yield. In particular, we analyzed a 4 percent real yield and a 3 percent real yield—the latter of which is a reasonable proxy for a riskless rate of return. We found that if returns were only 4 percent, the necessary contribution rate would rise to 13.4 percent, and if we used a risk-free return of roughly 3 percent, the necessary contribution rates would need to be much higher—nearly 18.1 percent of wages. On the other hand, if real returns were higher than our base-case level—perhaps 6 percent—the necessary contribution rate would only be only 4.4 percent, much lower than the current contribution rate.

Projections of Health Care Costs for State and Local Employees and Retirees

Most state and local governments pay for employee and retiree health insurance on a pay-as-you-go basis—that is, these benefits are generally not prefunded. We made projections of the pay-as-you-go expenditures for health care for the sector, as a percentage of wages, in each year until 2050.[12] To estimate expenditures for employee and retiree health insurance in future years, we made many of the same assumptions as for the pension analysis. In particular, we use the same method to develop projections of employment in the sector, the number of retirees, and the level of wages. An additional assumption for the health care analysis is that in future years, the same percentage of employees and retirees of state and local governments will be enrolled in health insurance through their previous employer as we observe were enrolled in 2004—the most recent year for which data were available. For retirees, we developed this measure from two data sources. The Census Bureau's State and Local Government Employee-Retirement System survey provided data on the total number of state and local retirees, and the Health and Human Services Department's Medical Expenditure Panel Survey (MEPS) provided data on state and local government retirees who are covered by employer-provided health insurance. Based on these data sources we found that the share of retirees with health insurance is 44 percent, and we hold this constant through the simulations. From the latter data source we also obtained the most recent year state and local government spending on health care for retirees. For active employees we also used MEPS data on employees covered by health insurance and compared that to BEA data on the total employment in the sector. This provided us with a finding that 71 percent of active employees are receiving health benefits. Again, we hold this value constant during the simulation time frame.

One of the most central assumptions we must make to estimate the pay-as-you-go health care expenditures for employees and retirees in future years is the cost growth of health care itself. The cost of health care has been increasing faster than gross domestic product (GDP) for many years. As such, we developed assumptions about how much faster health care costs would grow, relative to the economy, in future years. The extent to which the per-person cost of health care is expected to grow beyond GDP per capita is called the "excess cost factor." We developed these estimates based on our own research and discussions with experts. In particular, we assume that the excess cost factor averages 1.4 percentage points per year through 2035, and then begins to decline, reaching 0.6 percentage points by 2050.

Using these assumptions we developed projections for the expenditures on health care for employees and retirees each year through 2050. We found that the projected expenditures for retiree health insurance, while not a large component of state budgets, will more than double as a percentage of wages over the next several decades. In 2006, these expenditures amounted to approximately 2.1 percent of wages, and by 2050 we project that they will grow to nearly 5.1 percent of wages—a 150 percent increase. As with the projections of necessary pension contributions, our estimates of these expenditures are highly sensitive to certain of our assumptions. In particular, the assumptions regarding health care cost growth are critical. For example, if health costs were to only rise at the rate of GDP per capita, expenditures for retiree health care would only grow, as a percentage of wages, from 2.1 percent today to 3.0 percent by 2050. Conversely, if health costs were to grow by twice the rate we assume in the base case, these costs, as a percentage of wages, would constitute 8.7 percent by 2050.[13]

Active employees' expenditures on health care amounted to 12.8 percent of wages in 2006 and by the end of the simulations in 2050 are expected to be 22.2 percent of wages. In the case of the optimistic scenario—with lower escalation in the cost of health care—we found that expenditures on employee health care will only rise slightly to 13 percent of wages by 2050. However, under the pessimistic scenario characterized by more rapidly growing health costs, expenditures on health care for active employees rise to 37.7 percent of wages in 2050.

Appendix IV

STATE AND LOCAL MODEL EQUATIONS

This appendix lists the 105 equations that are used to simulate the base case for the State and Local Model.

Notation:

Variable(-X): Represents the variable lagged X periods.

(*Expression*>=0): Is an indicator term that is one when the expression evaluates to greater than zero and is zero otherwise.

AR(X): Indicates an auto-regressive of order X is included in the econometric specification.

MA(X): A moving average term of order X is included in the specification.

YEAR: The current year being forecasted.

PENSION EQUATIONS

1. EGSLALL = ((NP / NP(-1))) * EGSLALL(-1) * (LYFCST - YEAR>=0) + EGSLALL(-1) * (EGSLALL(-1) / EGSLALL(-2)) * (LYFCST - YEAR<0)
2. EGSLALL_HP = (EGSLALL / EGSLALL(-1)) * EGSLALL_HP(-1)
3. GSL = (EGSLALL / EGSLALL(-1)) * EGSL(-1)
4. DLOG(BENEFICIARIES) = 0.5594068 * DLOG(EGSLALL_HP(-34)) + 0.0003020 * DLOG(EGSLALL_HP(-25)) + 0.0002169 * DLOG(EGSLALL_HP(-24)) + 0.0225695 * DLOG(EGSLALL_HP(-23)) + 0.1913009 *

DLOG(EGSLALL_HP(-22)) + 0.2262039 * DLOG(EGSLALL_HP(-21))

5. JECISTLC = JECISTLC(-1) * (JECIWSP / JECIWSP(-1))
6. JECISTLCR = JECISTLCR(-1) * ((JECIWSP / JECIWSP(-1)) / (CPIU / CPIU(-1))) * (LYFCST - YEAR>=0) + JECISTLCR(-1) * (JECISTLCR(-1) / JECISTLCR(-2)) * (LYFCST - YEAR<0)
7. GSLCWAGEALLR = (GSLCWAGEALLR(-1) * (JECISTLCR / JECISTLCR(-1)) * (EGSLALL / EGSLALL(-1)))
8. GSLCWAGEALL = GSLCWAGEALL(-1) * (GSLCWAGEALLR / GSLCWAGEALLR(-1)) * (CPIU / CPIU(-1))
9. GSLCWAGE = (GSLCWAGE(-1)) * (JECISTLC / JECISTLC(-1)) * (EGSL / EGSL(-1))
10. PVGSLCWAGEALLR = GSLCWAGEALLR / (1 + (RPENREAL / 100))^(YEAR - LYACTUAL)
11. TPVGSLCWAGEALLR = PVGSLCWAGEALLR + TPVGSLCWAGEALLR(-1)
12. DEATHRATE = DEATHRATE(-1)
13. WN = (BENEFICIARIES - (1 - DEATHRATE(-1)) * BENEFICIARIES(-1)) / BENEFICIARIES
14. WC = BENEFICIARIES(-1) / BENEFICIARIES
15. WD = (DEATHRATE(-1) * BENEFICIARIES(-1) / BENEFICIARIES)
16. WJECISTLCR = WN * JECISTLCR + WC * JECISTLCR(-8) - WD * JECISTLCR(-21)
17. (PENBENR / BENEFICIARIES) = (PENBENR(-1) / BENEFICIARIES(-1)) * (WJECISTLCR / WJECISTLCR(-1))
18. PENBEN = PENBEN(-1) * (PENBENR / PENBENR(-1)) * (CPIU / CPIU(-1))
19. PVPENBENR = PENBENR / (1 + (RPENREAL / 100))^(YEAR - LYACTUAL)
20. TPVPENBENR = PVPENBENR + TPVPENBENR(-1)
21. EECONPENR / GSLCWAGEALLR = EECONPENR(-1) / GSLCWAGEALLR(-1)
22. EECONPEN / GSLCWAGEALL = EECONPEN(-1) / GSLCWAGEALL(-1)
23. PVEECONPENR = EECONPENR / (1 + (RPENREAL / 100))^(YEAR - LYACTUAL)
24. TPVEECONPENR = PVEECONPENR + TPVEECONPENR(-1)
25. L1TOTALFALYACT = L1TOTALFALYACT(-1)

26. TPVGSLCPEN = TPVPENBENR - L1TOTALFALYACT - TPVEECONPENR
27. GSLCPEN = (TPVGSLCPEN(2400)/ TPVGSLCWAGEALLR (2400))* GSLCWAGE
28. L1TOTALFA = L1TOTALFA(-1) * (1 + (RPENREAL / 100)) * (CPIU / CPIU(-1)) + EECONPEN + GSLCPEN - PENBEN

RECEIPTS

29. GSLRCPTC = TXGSL + TXSIGSL + YGSLA + YGSLTRF + SURGSLE
30. TXGSL = TXPGSL + TXIMGSLS + TXIMGSLPROP + TXIMGSLO + TXCORPGSL + EXOGTAXSHIFT
31. TXPGSLINC = TXPGSTATE + TXPGLOCAL
32. TXPGSL = TXPGSLINC + TXPGSLO
33. TXPGSTATE_RESID = TXPGSTATE_RESID(-1)
34. LOG(TXPGSTATE / (JPGDP / 100)) = - 4.663012457 + 1.106786257 * LOG(YPTAXABLE / (JPGDP / 100)) + TXPGSTATE_RESID
35. TXPGLOCAL = TXPGLOCAL(-1) * YPTAXABLE / YPTAXABLE (-1)
36. TXPGSLO = TXPGSLO(-1) * (YPTAXABLE / YPTAXABLE(-1))
37. CBASER_RESID = CBASER_RESID(-1)
38. LOG(CBASER) = - 0.356670 + 0.926710 * LOG(YPCOMPWSDR) + CBASER_RESID
39. CBASE = CBASER * (JPGDP / 100)
40. TXIMGSLS = TXIMGSLSGEN + TXIMGSLSOTH
41. TXIMGSLSGEN = TXIMGSLSGEN(-1) * (CBASE / CBASE(-1))
42. TXIMGSLSOTH_RESID = TXIMGSLSOTH_RESID(-1)
43. LOG(TXIMGSLSOTH / (JPGDP / 100)) = - 2.19455711 + 0.802359052* LOG(YPCOMPWSDR) + TXIMGSLSOTH_RESID
44. TXIMGSLPROP = TXIMGSLPROP(-1) * (REST_ALT / REST_ALT (-1))
45. RESTR_ALT_RESID = RESTR_ALT_RESID(-1)
46. LOG(RESTR_ALT) = - 0.3439280383 + 1.125733159 * LOG(GDPR) +RESTR_ALT_RESID
47. REST_ALT = RESTR_ALT * (JPGDP / 100)
48. TXIMGSLO = TXIMGSLO(-1) * (GDP / GDP(-1))

49. TXCORPGSL = TXCORPGSL(-1) * (ZB / ZB(-1))
50. TXSIGSL = TXSIGSL(-1) * (YPCOMPWSD/ YPCOMPWSD (-1))
51. YGSLA = (RATEASSETS / 100) * SLG_AFINL(-1)
52. RATEASSETS = 0.8110814608 * RATEASSETS(-1) + (1 - 0.8110814608) * RMTBM3 - 1.47259976 * D86
53. YGSLTRF = GFAIDSL + YGSLTRFBUS + YGSLTRFP
54. GFAIDSL = GFAIDSLO + (GFAIDSLSSMED - CLAWBACK)
55. CLAWBACK = CLAWBACKPER * GFAIDSLSSMED
56. YGSLTRFBUS = YGSLTRFBUS(-1) * (GDP / GDP(-1))
57. YGSLTRFP = YGSLTRFP(-1) * (GDP / GDP(-1))
58. SURGSLE = 0

Expenditures

59. GSLEXPC = GSLC + YPTRFGSL + GSLINTPAY + SUBGSL + EXOGEXPSHIFT
60. GSLC = GSLCWSS + GSLCKF + GSLCO
61. GSLCWSS = GSLCWAGE + GSLCPEN + GSLCHLTH + GSLCOTHBEN
62. GSLCHLTH = RETGSLCHLTH + EEGSLCHLTH
63. (EEGSLCHLTH / EGSLHLTH) = (EEGSLCHLTH (-1) / EGSLHLTH (-1)) * (HLTHNHEEXCGR) * ((GDP / NP) / (GDP(-1) / NP(-1)))
64. (RETGSLCHLTH / RETHLTH) = (RETGSLCHLTH (-1) / RETHLTH (-1)) * (HLTHNHEEXCGR) * ((GDP / NP) / (GDP(-1) / NP(-1)))
65. RETHLTH = RETHLTHPERBEN * BENEFICIARIES * (EGSL / EGSLALL)
66. RETHLTHPERBEN = RETHLTHPERBEN(-1)
67. EGSLHLTH = EGSL * (EGSLHLTH(-1) / EGSL(-1))
68. GSLCOTHBEN = GSLCOTHBEN(-1) * (JECISTLC / JECISTLC(-1)) * (EGSL / EGSL(-1))
69. GSLCO = GSLCO(-1) * (NP / NP(-1)) * (JPGDP / JPGDP(-1))
70. GSLGI = GSLGI(-1) * (NP / NP(-1)) * (JPGDP / JPGDP(-1))
71. GSLGIR = GSLGI / (JPGDP / 100)
72. KGSLR = KGSLR(-1) + GSLGIR - GSLCKFALLR
73. GSLCKFALLR = 0.027508 * KGSLR(-1)
74. GSLCKFALL = GSLCKFALLR * (JPGDP / 100)

75. GSLCKF = GSLCKF(-1) * (GSLCKFALL / GSLCKFALL(-1))
76. YPTRFGSL = YPTRFGSLPAM + YPTRFGSLPAO
77. YPTRFGSLPAM = 1.726 * GFAIDSLSSMED
78. YPTRFGSLPAO = YPTRFGSLPAO(-1) * (NP / NP (-1)) * (JPGDP / JPGDP (-1))

INTEREST RATES

79. RMMUNIAAA_RESID = RMMUNIAAA_RESID(-1)
80. RMMUNIAAA = 0.707151184659468 + 0.761815685970831 * RMTCM10Y + RMMUNIAAA_RESID
81. GSLINTPAY = (RATEOWED / 100) * SLG_LCRED(-1)
82. RATEOWED = 0.8765652676 * RATEOWED(-1) + (1 - 0.8765652676) * RMMUNIAAA
83. NETASSETPAY = GSLINTPAY - YGSLA
84. SUBGSL = SUBGSL(-1) * (NP / NP(-1)) * (JPGDP / JPGDP(-1))

BALANCE MEASURES AND INVESTMENT

85. NETSAVGSL = GSLRCPTC - GSLEXPC
86. NETSIGSL = NETSIGSL(-1) * (YPCOMPWSD / YPCOMPWSD (-1))
87. GSLRCPT = GSLRCPTC + GSLRCPTKTRF
88. GSLRCPTKTRF = IGRANT + ESTATETAX
89. IGRANT = IGRANT(-1) * (IGRANTCBO / IGRANTCBO(-1))
90. ESTATETAX = ESTATETAX(-1) * (1 + RMTCM10Y / 100)
91. GSLEXP = GSLEXPC + GSLGI + GSLNETPCHNA - GSLCKFALL
92. GSLNETPCHNA = GSLNETPCHNA(-1) * (JPGDP / JPGDP(-1)) * (NP / NP(-1))
93. NETLENDGSL = GSLRCPT - GSLEXP
94. OPBALNETCAP = GSLRCPT - (GSLGI + GSLNETPCHNA - D(DBTGSLLT)) - (GSLEXPC - GSLCKF) - SURGSLE - NETSIGSL

FINANCIAL ASSETS AND LIABILITIES

95. D(DBTGSLLT) / (GSLGI + GSLNETPCHNA - IGRANT) =0.478671765326665 - 0.0678320738849175 * D(RMMUNIAAA) +0.469267348080956 * D78 + 1.3549185597115 * D85 - 0.571578002864546 * D94 - 0.549417581324232 * D95 + [AR(1) =0.720101110280723]
96. D(DBTGSLST) / GDP = (0.000435862040461702 - 0.237982866875603 *D(NETSAVGSL) / GDP - 0.00116135948551944 * D75 -0.00305076556061719 * D76 - 0.00187119472727474 * D77 -0.00199332729108819 * D87 + [AR(1) = 0.419998514150027 , AR(3) =0.377010382422796 , MA(1) = - 0.378513568750189 , MA(2) =0.320241719235162 , MA(3) = - 0.93530313308922 , BACKCAST =1964]) * (1 - SLG_AFINLSWITCH(-1)) + ((D(SLG_AFINL) -D(DBTGSLLT) - D(TRADEPAYABLES) - D(DBTGSLUS) -NETLENDGSL) / (GDP)) * (SLG_AFINLSWITCH(-1))
97. DDBTGSLSTGDP_GRECON = (0.000435862040461702 - 0.237982866875603 * D(NETSAVGSL) / GDP - 0.00116135948551944 *D75 - 0.00305076556061719 * D76 - 0.00187119472727474 * D77 -0.00199332729108819 * D87 + [AR(1) = 0.419998514150027 , AR(3) =0.377010382422796 , MA(1) = - 0.378513568750189 , MA(2) =0.320241719235162 , MA(3) = - 0.93530313308922 , BACKCAST =1964])
98. DBTGSLTE = DBTGSLLT + DBTGSLST
99. 99. DLOG(DBTGSLUS / (JPGDP / 100)) = 0.026989088699108 -1.46693539308972 * DLOG(GDPR) + 0.671368273891861 * D84 +0.347532134271165 * D85 - 1.11842691662586 * D88 + [AR(2) = -0.304187166509849 , MA(1) = - 0.961550584145944 , BACKCAST =1970]
100. TRADEPAYABLES = TRADEPAYABLES(-1) * (GSLCO / GSLCO (-1))
101. SLG_LCRED = DBTGSLLT + DBTGSLST + DBTGSLUS
102. SLG_LFINL = SLG_LCRED + TRADEPAYABLES
103. SLG_AFINLSWITCH = ((SLG_AFINL/ SLG_AFINL(-1)) - (GDP/GDP(-1))<=0) * (YEAR>(LYACTUAL + 1)) * (DSLG_AFINL_GRALT / SLG_AFINL(-1) - (GDP/GDP(-1)-1)<=0)

104. SLG_AFINL_GRALT = GDP * DDBTGSLSTGDP_GRECON + D(DBTGSLLT) + D(TRADEPAYABLES) + D(DBTGSLUS) + NETLENDGSL

105. D(SLG_AFINL) = (NETLENDGSL + D(SLG_LFINL)) * (1 - SLG_AFINLSWITCH(-1)) + (SLG_AFINL(-1) * ((GDP / GDP(-1)) - 1)) * (SLG_AFINLSWITCH(-1))

Appendix V

ALPHABETICAL LIST OF STATE AND LOCAL SECTOR MODEL VARIABLES AND DEFINITIONS

This appendix describes the variables in the state and local model as well as their sources.

BENEFICIARIES = Total retired state and local government beneficiaries receiving periodic benefit payments, thousands; Census Bureau Government Retirement System. Values prior to 1981 are imputed using a constant growth rate between available data.

CBASE = Personal consumption less food, services, electronic and mail-order sales, billions of dollars; U.S. Commerce Department, Bureau of Economic Analysis NIPA table 2.3.5 lines 1 - 7 - 13 less Census Current Business Reports, Annual Revision of Monthly Retail and Food Services: Sales and Inventories—January 1992 Through February 2006 Table 2 NAICS code 4541 (for 1992 and later years) http://www.census.gov/prod/www/abs/br_month.html or Census Historical Retail Trade Data (SIC-Based) http://www.census.gov/mrts/ www/ mrtshist.html SIC code 5961 (through 1991).

CBASER = Real personal consumption less food, services, electronic and mail-order sales, billions of 2000 dollars; calculated by GAO.

CBASER_RESID = Residual from the sales tax base equation, calculated by GAO.

CELECMAIL = Electronic and mail order sales, billions of dollars; Census Bureau NAICS 4541 for 1992 – 2006, SIC Code 5961 for 1978–1991 and estimated with an exponential function for 1960–1977.

CLAWBACK = Payments from states to the federal government related to the savings incurred as part of Medicare Part D, billions of dollars; CBO, The Budget and Economic Outlook (Washington, D.C.: January 2007) Box 3-2.

CLAWBACKPER = Payments from states to the federal government related to the savings incurred as part of Medicare Part D, as a percentage of Medicaid Grants from the Federal Government; calculated by GAO.

CPIU=Consumer price index all urban, index 1982 - 1984 = 100; CBO, The Budget and Economic Outlook: An Update (Washington, D.C.: August 2007), Table C-1.

Di = Dummy variable; 1 in year i, 0 in other years.

DBTGSLLT = Medium and long-term municipal securities outstanding, billions of dollars; Board of Governors of the Federal Reserve System, Flow of Funds Table L.105 line 22.

DBTGSLST = Short-term municipal securities outstanding, billions of dollars; Board of Governors of the Federal Reserve System, Flow of Funds Table L.105 line 21.

DBTGSLTE = Municipal securities outstanding, billions of dollars; Board of Governors of the Federal Reserve System, Flow of Funds Table L.105 line 20.

DBTGSLUS = U.S. Government loans to state and local governments outstanding, billions of dollars; Board of Governors of the Federal Reserve System, Flow of Funds Table L.105 line 23.

DDBTGSLSTGDP_GRECON = Projected growth in short-term municipal securities outstanding based on econometric specification, percentage of GDP; calculated by GAO.

DEATHRATE = Percentage of OASDI beneficiaries that have been terminated; Calculated by the GAO as terminated OASDI beneficiaries from SSA table 6.F1 and total OASDI beneficiaries from table 5.A4. Missing values imputed with a constant growth rate.

DEPRATE = Consumption of fixed capital, as a percentage of the prior period's net capital stock of state and local governments; calculated by the GAO as GSLCKFALLR/KGSLR(-1).

DSLG_AFINL_GRALT = Alternate projection of the change in total financial assets of state and local governments based on econometric projection of short-term municipal securities outstanding, billions of dollars; calculated by GAO.

EECONPEN = Aggregate pension contributions by state and local employees, billions of dollars; U.S. Commerce Department, Bureau of

Economic Analysis NIPA Table 6.11A, 6.11B and 6.11C Line 50 and 6.11D Line 52.

EECONPENR = Aggregate pension contributions by state and local employees, billions of dollars deflated by the consumer price index; calculated by GAO.

EEGSLCHLTH = State and local government health care contributions for active employees, billions of dollars; U.S. Department of Health and Human Services, Agency for Healthcare Research and Quality, Medical Expenditure Panel Survey.

ESTATETAX = State and local government estate and gift taxes paid by persons, billions of dollars; U.S. Department of Commerce, Bureau of Economic Analysis, NIPA table 5.10 line 9.

EGSL = State and local general government employees, thousands; U.S. Department of Commerce, Bureau of Economic Analysis Table 6.4A, 6.4B, and 6.4C. Full-Time and Part-Time Employees by Industry line 83 and 6.4D Full-Time and Part-Time Employees by Industry line 93.

EGSLALL = State and local government employees, thousands; U.S. Department of Commerce, Bureau of Economic Analysis Table 6.4A, 6.4B and 6.4C Full-Time and Part-Time Employees by Industry line 82 and 6.4D Full-Time and Part-Time Employees by Industry line 92.

EGSLALL_HP = Hodrick-Prescott filtered series of EGSLALL, thousands; calculated by GAO.

EGSLHLTH = State and local government employees receiving health care benefits, thousands; U.S. Department of Health and Human Services, Agency for Healthcare Research and Quality, Medical Expenditure Panel Survey.

EXOGEXPSHIFT = Exogenous change in expenditures for state and local governments. Variable is zero in baseline scenario and non-zero in sensitivities involving alternative expenditures, billions of dollars; calculated by GAO.

EXOGTAXSHIFT = Exogenous change in tax revenue for state and local governments. Variable is zero in baseline scenario and non-zero in sensitivities involving alternative tax revenues, billions of dollars; calculated by GAO.

GDP = Gross domestic product, billions of dollars; U.S. Department of Commerce, Bureau of Economic Analysis, NIPA Table 1.1.5 line 1; exogenous, projections from CBO, The Budget and Economic Outlook: An Update (Washington, D.C.: August 2007), Table C-1.

GDPR = Gross domestic product, billions of chained 2000 dollars; U.S. Department of Commerce, Bureau of Economic Analysis, NIPA Table

1.1.6 line 1; exogenous, projections from CBO, The Budget and Economic Outlook: An Update (Washington, D.C.: August 2007), Table C-1.

GFAIDSL = Federal grants-in-aid to state and local governments, billions of dollars; U.S. Department of Commerce, Bureau of Economic Analysis, NIPA Table 3.3 line 17; exogenous, projections from CBO, The Treatment of Federal Receipts and Expenditures in the National Income and Product Accounts (Washington, D.C.: August 2007) Table 2; interpolated from fiscal to calendar year by GAO.

GFAIDSLO = Federal non-Medicaid grants to state and local governments, billions of dollars; calculated by GAO using U.S. Department of Commerce data as the difference between GFAIDSL and GFAIDSLSSMED; exogenous projection values calculated in the same way.

GFAIDSLSSMED = Federal Medicaid grants, billions of dollars; U.S. Department of Commerce, Bureau of Economic Analysis, NIPA Table 3.21U line 12; exogenous, projections from CBO, The Budget and Economic Outlook: An Update (Washington, D.C.: August 2007) Table 1-4 and CBO, The Long-Term Budget Outlook (Washington, D.C.: December 2005), p. 31 and http://www.cbo.gov/ftpdocs/69xx/doc6982/Data.xls.

GSLC = Total consumption expenditures of state and local governments, billions of dollars; U.S. Department of Commerce, Bureau of Economic Analysis, NIPA Table 3.3 line 22.

GSLCHLTH = State and local government health benefit contributions, billions of dollars; U.S. Department of Health and Human Services, Agency for Healthcare Research and Quality, Medical Expenditure Panel Survey.

GSLCKF = Consumption of general government fixed capital, billions of dollars; U.S. Department of Commerce, Bureau of Economic Analysis, NIPA table 3.10.5 line 51.

GSLCKFALL = Consumption of fixed capital, billions of dollars; U.S. Department of Commerce, Bureau of Economic Analysis, NIPA table 3.3 line 38.

GSLCKFALLR= Consumption of fixed capital, billions of 2000 dollars; GAO calculation for years through 2006 = 2000 nominal value from U.S. Department of Commerce, Bureau of Economic Analysis, NIPA Fixed Asset Table 7.3B line 46 times the relevant year's quantity index/100 from NIPA Fixed Asset Table 7.4B line 46.

GSLCKFALL = Government consumption of fixed capital, billions of dollars; U.S. Department of Commerce, Bureau of Economic Analysis, NIPA table 3.3 line 38.

GSLCO = State and local consumption excluding employee compensation and capital consumption, billions of dollars; U.S. Department of Commerce, Bureau of Economic Analysis, calculated by GAO as GSLCO = GSLC-GSLCWSS-GSLCKF.

GSLCOTHBEN = Other general state and local government employee compensation, billions of dollars; calculated by GAO from U.S. Department of Commerce, Bureau of Economic Analysis, total compensation less the sum of wages and salary accruals, pension contributions and health benefits (GSLCOTHBEN= GSLCWSS-GSLCWAGE-GSLCPEN-GSLCHLTH).

GSLCPEN = State and local government contribution for general government employees, billions of dollars; U.S. Department of Commerce, Bureau of Economic Analysis, calculated by GAO based on NIPA tables 7.8 and 6.3A, 6.3B, 6.3C and 6.3D.

GSLCPENALL = State and local government contribution for general and enterprise employees, billions of dollars; U.S. Department of Commerce, Bureau of Economic Analysis, NIPA table 7.8 Line 10.

GSLCWSS = Total compensation for state and local government employees, billions of dollars; U.S. Department of Commerce, Bureau of Economic Analysis, NIPA table 3.10.5 line 50.

GSLCWAGE = State and local wages for general government employees, billions of dollars; U.S. Department of Commerce, Bureau of Economics Analysis, NIPA table 6.3A, 6.3B, 6.3C Line 83 and 6.3D Line 93.

GSLCWAGEALL = Total state and local wages for general government and government enterprise employees, billions of dollars; U.S. Department of Commerce, Bureau of Economics Analysis, NIPA table 6.3A, 6.3B, 6.3C Line 82 and 6.3D Line 92.

GSLCWAGEALLR = Total state and local wages for general and enterprise government employees deflated by the consumer price index, billions of 2006 dollars; calculated by GAO.

GSLEXP = Total expenditures of state and local governments, billions of dollars; U.S. Department of Commerce, Bureau of Economic Analysis, NIPA Table 3.3 line 33.

GSLEXPC = Total current expenditures of state and local governments, billions of dollars; U.S. Department of Commerce, Bureau of Economic Analysis, NIPA Table 3.3 line 21.

GSLGI = Gross investment of state and local governments, billions of dollars; U.S. Department of Commerce, Bureau of Economic Analysis, NIPA table 3.3 line 35.

GSLGIR = Gross investment of state and local governments, billions of chained 2000 dollars; U.S. Department of Commerce, Bureau of Economic Analysis, NIPA table 3.9.6 line 23.

GSLINTPAY = Interest paid by state and local governments, billions of dollars; U.S. Department of Commerce, Bureau of Economic Analysis, NIPA Table 3.3 line 24

GSLNETPCHNA = Net purchases of non-produced assets by state and local governments, billions of dollars; U.S. Department of Commerce, Bureau of Economic Analysis, NIPA Table 3.3 line 37.

GSLRCPT = Total receipts of state and local governments, billions of dollars; U.S. Department of Commerce, Bureau of Economic Analysis, NIPA Table 3.3 line 30

GSLRCPTC = Total current receipts of state and local governments, billions of dollars; U.S. Department of Commerce, Bureau of Economic Analysis, NIPA Table 3.3 line 1.

GSLRCPTKTRF= Capital transfers received (net), state and local governments, billions of dollars; U.S. Department of Commerce, Bureau of Economic Analysis, NIPA Table 3.3 line 32.

HIMEDRATIO = Federal Medicaid spending as a percentage of GDP, high cost scenario, percentage; CBO, The Long-Term Budget Outlook (Washington, D.C.: December 2005) http://www.cbo.gov/ftpdocs/69xx/doc6982/Data.xls scenario 1.

HLTHNHEEXCGR = Multiplier reflecting the difference between growth in National Health Expenditures Spending per capita and growth in GDP per capita; GAO Analysis.

IGRANT = Federal investment grants to state and local governments, billions of dollars; U.S. Department of Commerce, Bureau of Economic Analysis, NIPA Table 5.10U line 9.

IGRANTCBO = Federal capital transfers; exogenous projections, billions of dollars; CBO, The Treatment of Federal Receipts and Expenditures in the National Income and Product Accounts (Washington, D.C.: August 2007) Table 1; interpolated from fiscal to calendar year by GAO.

JECIWSP = Employment cost index – private wages and salaries, 2005Q4=100.0; BLS Employment Cost Index Historical Index Table 6; exogenous, projections from CBO, The Budget and Economic Outlook: An Update (Washington, D.C.: August 2007), Table C-1.

JECISTLC=Employment cost index for state and local workers; 2005Q4=100.0, index; BLS Employment Cost Index Historical Index Table 6 (ftp://ftp.bls.gov/pub/suppl/eci.echistry.txt).

JECISTLCR=Employment cost index for state and local workers, deflated by the CPIU, index; calculated by GAO.

JPGDP = Chained price index - gross domestic product, index 2000=100; U.S. Department of Commerce, Bureau of Economic Analysis, NIPA table 1.1.4 line 1; exogenous, projections from The Budget and Economic Outlook: An Update (Washington, D.C.: August 2007), Table C-1.

KGSLR = Net capital stock of state and local governments, billions of 2000 dollars; U.S. Department of Commerce, Bureau of Economic Analysis, Fixed Asset Summary Table 9.1 line 21.

L1TOTALFA = Total state and local government employee retirement fund assets, billions of dollars; Board of Governors of the Federal Reserve System, Flow of Funds Table L.119 line 1.

L1TOTALFALYACT = Total state and local government employee retirement fund assets for the last year that actuals are available, billions of dollars; Board of Governors of the Federal Reserve System, Flow of Funds Table L.119 line 1.

LOWMEDRATIO = Federal Medicaid spending as a percentage of GDP low cost scenario, percentage; CBO, The Long-Term Budget Outlook (Washington, D.C.: December 2005) http://www.cbo.gov/ftpdocs/69xx/doc6982/Data.xls scenario 3.

LYACTUAL = last year actual data are available, 2006

LYFCST = last year of the forecast period, 2080.

NETASSETPAY = Interest payments less receipts on assets, billions of dollars; calculated by GAO as GSLINTPAY-YGSLA.

NETLENDGSL = Net lending or net borrowing (-) of state and local governments, billions of dollars; U.S. Department of Commerce, Bureau of Economic Analysis, NIPA Table 3.3 line 39.

NETSAVGSL = State and local government net saving, billions of dollars; U.S. Department of Commerce, Bureau of Economic Analysis, NIPA Table 3.3 line 27.

NETSIGSL = Net social insurance fund balance, billions of dollars; U.S. Department of Commerce, Bureau of Economic Analysis, NIPA Table 3.3 Line 28.

NP = Total population, thousands; exogenous projections 2007 OASDI Trustees Report, Table V.A2.-Social Security Area Population.

OPBALNETCAP= GAO's measure of the operating balance, excludes receipts used to acquire capital as well as capital-related expenditures; the balance also excludes the surplus/deficit of government enterprises and the net balance of social insurance funds, billions of dollars.

PENBEN= Aggregate pension payments made to state and local pension beneficiaries, billions of dollars; U.S. Department of Commerce, Bureau of Economic Analysis, NIPA table 6.11A, 6.11B, and 6.11C line 41 and 6.11D line 43.

PENBENR= Aggregate pension payments made to state and local pension beneficiaries deflated by the consumer price index, billions of 2000 dollars, calculated by GAO.

PVEECONPENR = Present value of EECONPENR using RPENREAL for each year; calculated by GAO.

PVGSLCWAGEALLR = Present value of GSLCWAGEALLR using RPENREAL for each year; calculated by GAO.

PVPENBENR = Present value of PENBENR using RPENREAL for each year; calculated by GAO.

RATEASSETS = Effective rate received on state and local government financial assets, interest rate; historical values calculated by GAO as RATEASSETS = 100*YGSLA / SLG_AFINL(-1).

RATEOWED = Effective rate paid on state and local government credit market instruments outstanding, interest rate; historical values calculated by GAO as RATEOWED = 100*GSLINTPAY / SLG_LCRED(-1).

REST_ALT = Market value of real estate and other property outstanding excluding business equipment at the end of the period, billions of dollars; Board of Governors of the Federal Reserve System, Flow of Funds Table B.100 line 4 plus B.102 line 3 plus B.103 line 3.

RESTR_ALT = Real market value of real estate and other property outstanding excluding business equipment at the end of the period, billions of chained 2000 dollars, calculated by GAO.

RESTR_ALT_RESID = Residual from the real estate tax base equation, calculated by GAO.

RETGSLCHLTH = State and local government health care contributions for retired employees, billions of dollars; U.S. Department of Health and Human Services, Agency for Healthcare Research and Quality, Medical Expenditure Panel Survey.

RETHLTH = State and local government retirees receiving healthcare benefits, thousands; U.S. Department of Health and Human Services, Agency for Healthcare Research and Quality, Medical Expenditure Panel Survey.

RETHLTHPERBEN = State and local government health care retired enrollees as a percentage of beneficiaries; calculated by GAO.

RMMUNIAAA = Rate on Aaa-rated municipal bonds, percent per annum; Board of Governors of the Federal Reserve System, Statistical Release H.15: Selected Interest Rates http://www.federalreserve.gov/releases/h15/data.htm.

RMMUNIAAA_RESID = Residual from the municipal rate equation, calculated by GAO.

RMTBM3= Yield on 3 month treasury bill, percent per annum; Board of Governors of the Federal Reserve System, Statistical Release H.15: Selected Interest Rates http://www.federalreserve.gov/releases/h15/data.htm. Exogenous, projections from CBO, The Budget and Economic Outlook: An Update (Washington, D.C.: August 2007), Table C-1.

RMTCM10Y= Yield on 10-year Treasury notes, percent per annum; Board of Governors of the Federal Reserve System, Statistical Release H.15: Selected Interest Rates http://www.federalreserve.gov/releases/h15 data.htm; exogenous, projections from CBO, The Budget and Economic Outlook: An Update (Washington, D.C.: August 2007), Table C-1.

RPENREAL = Real return on pension assets, interest rate; calculated by GAO as the sum of the product of the average real return from 1965 through 2005 (from Federal Reserve Board H.15 and other sources) on each retirement fund asset category (Flow of Funds table L.119) and each asset category's average share of assets over the last ten years = 5.0%.

SLG_AFINL = Total financial assets of state and local governments, billions of dollars; Board of Governors of the Federal Reserve System, Flow of Funds Table L.105 line 1.

SLG_AFINLSWITCH = One if assets grow slower than GDP when debt grows with econometric estimations, zero otherwise, dummy variable; calculated by GAO.

SLG_LCRED = Credit market instrument liabilities of state and local governments, billions of dollars; Board of Governors of the Federal Reserve System, Flow of Funds Table L.105 line 19.

SLG_LFINL = Total liabilities of state and local governments, billions of dollars; Board of Governors of the Federal Reserve System, Flow of Funds Table L.105 line 18.

SUBGSL = State and local government subsidy payments, billions of dollars; U.S. Department of Commerce, Bureau of Economic Analysis, NIPA Table 3.3 line 25.

SURGSLE = Current surplus of state and local government enterprises, billions of dollars; U.S. Department of Commerce, Bureau of Economic Analysis, NIPA Table 3.3 line 20.

TPVEECONPENR = Running sum of PVEECONPENR, billions of discounted dollars; calculated by GAO.

TPVGSLCPEN = Unfunded pension liability through a given year, billions of discounted dollars; calculated by GAO.

TPVGSLCWAGEALLR = Running sum of PVGSLCWAGEALLR, billions of discounted dollars; calculated by GAO.

TPVPENBENR = Running sum of PVPENBENR, billions of discounted dollars; calculated by GAO.

TRADEPAYABLES = Trade payables of state and local governments outstanding, billions of dollars; Board of Governors of the Federal Reserve System, Flow of Funds Table L.105 line 24.

TXCORPGSL = Taxes on corporate income, state and local governments, billions of dollars; U.S. Department of Commerce, Bureau of Economic Analysis, NIPA Table 3.3 line 10.

TXGSL = Current tax receipts, state and local governments, billions of dollars; U.S. Department of Commerce, Bureau of Economic Analysis, NIPA Table 3.3 line 2.

TXIMGSL = Taxes on production and imports, state and local governments, billions of dollars; U.S. Department of Commerce, Bureau of Economic Analysis, NIPA Table 3.3, line 6.

TXIMGSLO = Other taxes on production and imports, state and local governments, billions of dollars; U.S. Department of Commerce, Bureau of Economic Analysis, NIPA Table 3.3, line 9.

TXIMGSLPROP = Property tax receipts, state and local governments, billions of dollars; U.S. Department of Commerce, Bureau of Economic Analysis, NIPA Table 3.3, line 8.

TXIMGSLS = Sales tax receipts, state and local governments, billions of dollars; U.S. Department of Commerce, Bureau of Economic Analysis, NIPA Table 3.3, line 7.

TXIMGSLSGEN = General sales tax receipts, state and local governments, billions of dollars; U.S. Department of Commerce, Bureau of Economic Analysis, NIPA Table 3.5, lines 16 and 24.

TXIMGSLSOTH = Other sales tax receipts, state and local governments, billions of dollars; U.S. Department of Commerce, Bureau of Economic Analysis, NIPA Table 3.5, line 14 less 16 and 24.

TXIMGSLSOTH_RESID = Residual from the other sales tax receipts equation, calculated by GAO.

TXPGLOCAL = Local personal income tax receipts, billions of dollars; U.S. Department of Commerce, Bureau of Economic Analysis, NIPA Table 3.21 Line 4.

TXPGSL = Personal tax receipts, state and local governments, billions of dollars; U.S. Department of Commerce, Bureau of Economic Analysis, NIPA Table 3.3 line 3.

TXPGSLINC = Personal income tax receipts, state and local governments, billions of dollars; U.S. Department of Commerce, Bureau of Economic Analysis, NIPA Table 3.3 line 4.

TXPGSLO = Other personal tax receipts, state and local governments, billions of dollars; U.S. Department of Commerce, Bureau of Economic Analysis, NIPA Table 3.3 line 5.

TXPGSTATE = State personal income tax receipts, billions of dollars; U.S. Department of Commerce, Bureau of Economic Analysis, NIPA Table 3.20 Line 4.

TXPGSTATE_RESID = Residual from the state personal income tax receipts equation; calculated by GAO.

TXSIGSL = Contributions for government social insurance, state and local governments, billions of dollars; U.S. Department of Commerce, Bureau of Economic Analysis, NIPA Table 3.3 line 11.

WALDGSL = Wage accruals less disbursements, state and local government, billions of dollars; U.S. Department of Commerce, Bureau of Economic Analysis, NIPA Table 3.3 line 26.

WC = Weight of current beneficiaries. Last year beneficiaries as a share of current year beneficiaries, percentage; calculated by GAO.

WD = Weight of deceased beneficiaries. Number of deceased beneficiaries as a share of current year beneficiaries, percentage; calculated by GAO.

WJECISTLCR = Weighted real state and local employment cost index. Serves as a proxy for the growth in the average pension benefit, index; calculated by GAO.

WN = Weight of new beneficiaries. New beneficiaries as a share of total beneficiaries, percentage; calculated by GAO.

YGSLA = Income receipts on assets, state and local governments, billions of dollars; U.S. Department of Commerce, Bureau of Economic Analysis, NIPA Table 3.3 line 12.

YGSLTRF = Current transfer receipts, state and local governments, billions of dollars; U.S. Department of Commerce, Bureau of Economic Analysis, NIPA Table 3.3 line 16.

YGSLTRFBUS = Current transfer receipts from businesses, state and local governments, billions of dollars; U.S. Department of Commerce, Bureau of Economic Analysis, NIPA Table 3.3 line 18.

YGSLTRFP = Current transfer receipts from persons, state and local governments, billions of dollars; U.S. Department of Commerce, Bureau of Economic Analysis, NIPA Table 3.3 line 19.

YPCOMPWSD = Wage and salary disbursements, billions of dollars, U.S. Department of Commerce, Bureau of Economic Analysis, NIPA Table 2.1 line 3; exogenous, projections from CBO, The Budget and Economic Outlook: An Update (Washington, D.C.: August 2007), Table C-1.

YPCOMPWSDR = Real wage and salary disbursements, billions of chained 2000 dollars; calculated by GAO.

YPTAXABLE = Taxable personal income, billions of dollars. Calculated by GAO as wage and salary disbursements + dividends + interest + proprietors' income + rental income from U.S. Department of Commerce, Bureau of Economic Analysis, NIPA Table 2.1 lines 9, 12, 14 and 15; exogenous projections from CBO Budget and Economic Outlook.

YPTRFGSL = State and local social benefit payments to individuals, billions of dollars; U.S. Department of Commerce, Bureau of Economic Analysis, NIPA Table 3.3 line 23.

YPTRFGSLPAM = State and local medical spending on behalf of individuals, billions of dollars; U.S. Department of Commerce, Bureau of Economic Analysis, NIPA Table 3.12 line 32.

YPTRFGSLPAO = State and local non-medical social benefit payments to individuals, billions of dollars; calculated by GAO as YPTRFGSL – YPTRFGSLPAM.

ZB = Before-tax corporate profits excluding IVA, billions of dollars; U.S. Department of Commerce, Bureau of Economic Analysis, NIPA Table 1.12 line 44; exogenous projections from CBO, The Budget and Economic Outlook: An Update (Washington, D.C.: August 2007), Table C-1.

REFERENCES

[1] We previously provided a summary of this work. See State and Local Governments: Persistent Fiscal Challenges Will Likely Emerge within the Next Decade, GAO-07-1080SP (Washington, D.C.: July 2007).

[2] The federal unified budget is a comprehensive budget in which receipts and outlays from both federal funds and trust funds (e.g., Social Security) are consolidated.

[3] The state and local fiscal model is not designed for certain types of analyses. The simulations are not intended to provide precise predictions. Even though we know that these governments regularly make changes in tax laws and expenditures, the model essentially holds current policy in place and analyzes the fiscal future for the sector as if those policies were maintained because it would be highly speculative to make any assumptions about future policy adjustments.

[4] See GAO, The Nation's Long-Term Fiscal Outlook: August 2007 Update, GAO-07-1261R (Washington D.C.: August 2007).

[5] The count of general local governments includes the District of Columbia and excludes Indian tribes and outlying areas.

[6] To develop values for "unusual capital gains," we estimated a relationship between the level of capital gains over time and marginal tax rates. We viewed any observed gains (or losses), relative to the estimated relationship, as "unusual."

[7] Advances in productivity across types of production processes vary considerably. It is commonly believed that more labor-intensive outputs suffer from lower rates of productivity growth. This so-called "Baumol effect" may indicate that increases in productivity in

the provision of public services, such as public hospitals and education, tend to be low because these services rely so heavily on labor.

[8] CBO provides estimates of these private wage increases as measured by the employment cost index (ECI). The ECI grows about 1 percent per annum faster than the Consumer Price Index (CPI).

[9] Fiscal gap is calculated for the years 2007 to 2080.

[10] For Medicaid, our cost growth projections align with CBO's most recent budget baseline for the first 10 years and are based on CBO's December 2005 long-term projections in the later years.

[11] We developed estimates of cost growth for health insurance based on research and discussions with experts.

[12] In addition to expenses related to health care, the interest payments that state and local governments will need to make on their outstanding debt are also projected to grow substantially during the projection time frame, but this finding is merely an outgrowth of the sustained deficits the model predicts across future years.

[13] In fact, because the school age population is projected to decline as a proportion of the total population, we ran alternative simulations to examine outcomes with slower employment growth than the growth projected using the base case. We adjusted the growth in state and local employees to take into account slower growing school age populations in future years. This slowed the projected cost increases for compensation of state and local workers—a very large expenditure classification. As a result, operating balance deficits first appear 5 years later than in our base case. Although this led to a slower decline in fiscal balances, it did not avoid declining balances in the long run.

[14] Because CBO's baseline adjusts discretionary spending, such as non-Medicaid grants to state and local governments, only for inflation, our projections for these grants decline as a share of GDP over the next 10 years—the time frame of CBO's projections. Beyond that, we grow these expenditures at the rate of population growth plus inflation.

[15] In our simulations that combine the fiscal outcomes for all levels of government, the methodology underlying the federal simulations differs slightly from our past approach. Our federal budget simulations have incorporated the negative effect on economic growth of large deficits that divert funds from private investment. In order to combine the federal and state and local budget simulations

using a consistent set of economic assumptions, this feedback from deficits to economic growth is removed. With or without feedback, the simulations imply that fiscal policy is unsustainable over the long term.

[16] CBO, The Budget and Economic Outlook: An Update (Washington, D.C.: August 2007).

[17] For a description of the method applied to tax bases rather than receipts, see Russell S. Sobel and Randall G. Holcombe, "Measuring the Growth and Variability of Tax Bases over the Business Cycle," *National Tax Journal* 49 No. 4 (December 1996): 535-52. While following this method generally, for our work we only use the long-run elasticity described in these studies and not the full error-correction model which also takes into consideration the short-run cyclical changes.

[18] Suppose, for example, that the estimated long-run elasticity is 1.2 and the economy has been growing at a steady 3.0 percent for a number of years. The long-run elasticity of 1.2 implies that the trend growth in receipts is 3.6 percent (1.2 * 3.0).

[19] See Richard F. Dye and Therese J. McGuire, "Growth and Variablility of State Individual Income and General Sales Taxes," *National Tax Journal*, Vol. 44, No. 1 (1991), and Russell S. Sobel and Randall G. Holcombe, "Measuring the Growth and Variability of Tax Bases Over the Business Cycle," *National Tax Journal*, Vol. 49, No. 4 (1996).

[20] See CBO, Budget and Economic Outlook (August 2007).

[21] See CBO, *Long Term Budget Outlook* (December 2005).

Appendix II

[22] The changes in the sector's financial assets and liabilities are in Federal Reserve flow of funds table F.105 and the corresponding outstanding levels are in table L.105.

Appendix III

[23] In 2007 we issued State and Local Government Retiree Benefits: Current Status of Benefit Structures, Protections, and Fiscal Outlook for Funding Future Costs, GAO-07-1156 (Washington, D.C.:

September 2007), in which we provided estimates of pension and health costs for state and local government retirees based on data available at that time. Since then, the annual revision of the NIPA as well as the Medical Expenditure Panel Survey (MEPS) of the Department of Health and Human Services became available. The results presented in this report reflect those updates.

[24] See The 2007 Annual Report of the Board of Trustees of the Federal Old-Age and Survivors Insurance and Disability Insurance Trust Funds (Washington, D.C.: May 1, 2007), Table A2.

[25] This assumption implies that if there were no growth in the productivity of state and local workers, the output of services per person served would remain the same. As such, any increased growth in services provided per citizen hinges on the degree to which productivity in public sector services advances.

[26] CPI data are from CBO, *The Budget and Economic Outlook: An Update* (Washington, D.C.: August 2007). These data are available through 2017. For later years, we hold the growth rate constant at the rate that CBO assumes between 2016 and 2017.

[27] The Excel Solver function was used to find the weights that minimized the sum of the squared residuals between actual and fitted beneficiaries.

[28] See *Annual Statistical Supplement to the Social Security Bulletin, 2005* (Washington, D.C.: February 2006), Table 6.F1 Number of benefits terminated, by type, 1940–2004.

[29] See *Annual Statistical Supplement to the Social Security Bulletin, 2005* (Washington, D.C.: February 2006), Table 5.A4 Number and total monthly benefits, by trust fund and type of benefit, December 1940–2004, selected years.

[30] We use a constant death rate throughout our simulation analysis, but the Social Security Administration is actually projecting a decline in death rate during this time frame.

[31] The starting value of pension assets for state and local government pension plans—in 2006—is obtained from the Federal Reserve Flow of Funds Accounts.

[32] Public pension funds hold substantial assets, amounting to $3.0 trillion at year-end 2006. Because the calculation we make implies that all assets are used to pay benefits, the estimated contribution rate would be negative over short intervals. But, in fact, some of the assets already in the pension funds are related to liabilities that will not be paid for many years into the future. As the time horizon

increases, the present value of liabilities grows relative to assets, resulting in an increase in the estimated contribution rate. When the projection horizon lengthens sufficiently, however, the contribution rate stabilizes. That is, at some point there is virtually no difference in contribution rates estimated over successively longer projection periods. A 400-year projection horizon is long enough to provide an estimated contribution rate invariant to further increases in the projection period. The result is an estimate of the contribution rate necessary to fund pension payments on a sustainable basis.

[33] When evaluating state and local government pensions, standard practice is to use a discount rate based on the expected rate of return on pension fund investments. To develop a measure of the expected pension return, we analyzed data from Flow of Funds Accounts table L.119 (State and Local Employee Government Retirement Funds). We calculated each asset category's annual share of total fund assets and assigned a rate of return to each category. The asset groups included money-like assets (sum of checkable deposits and currency, time and savings deposits, money market mutual funds, and repurchase agreement securities (RPs), open market paper, treasury securities, agency- and government-sponsored enterprise- (GSE) backed securities, municipal securities, corporate and foreign bonds, mortgages, corporate equities, mutual fund shares, and other miscellaneous assets). Although data are available beginning in 1952 for pension fund assets, yields for all of the asset categories are only available starting in 1965. Accordingly, for each year from 1965 through 2005 we calculated the weighted average nominal return by summing the product of each asset's share and its return. Factoring out each year's CPIU increase provides an estimate of the real pension fund return. Because there has been a long-term shift in pension fund portfolios away from fixed income assets toward equities, the average real return over this period is not representative of likely future returns. To find an estimated real pension yield more representative of the recent composition of retirement fund investments, we used the average asset shares during the most recent 10-year period as portfolio weights. Multiplying these 10-year weights by each asset category's average real return over the entire period from 1965 through 2005 and summing the products results in an estimated real pension return of 5.0 percent. In our base case, therefore, we use a real discount rate of 5.0 percent to find the present value of future cash flows.

[34] Implicitly we assume that the medical coverage continues to pay about the same percentage of medical costs for employees and retirees as it currently does.

[35] Because our state and local government retiree health care cost estimates are based on data that did not incorporate possible savings attributable to the Medicare part D drug subsidy that began in 2006, the estimates may overstate retiree health slightly.

INDEX

D

E

R

S

T

U

V

W

Y